INDEPENDENT WOMEN

INDEPENDENT WOMEN

The Function of Gender in the Novels of Barbara Pym

Edited by

JANICE ROSSEN

Assistant Professor of English
Illinois Wesleyan University

THE HARVESTER PRESS · SUSSEX
ST. MARTIN'S PRESS · NEW YORK

First published 1988 by
The Harvester Press Ltd,
16 Ship Street, Brighton,
Sussex BN1 1AD
A Division of
Simon & Schuster International Group

and in the USA by
St. Martin's Press Inc.,
175 Fifth Avenue,
New York, NY 10010

Printed and bound in Great Britain by
Billings & Sons Ltd, Worcester

British Library Cataloguing in Publication Data

Independent women : the function of gender
in the novels of Barbara Pym.
1. Fiction in English. Pym, Barbara—
Critical studies
I. Rossen, Janice, *1955*–
823'.914
ISBN 0–7108–1287–6

Library of Congress Cataloging-in-Publication Data

Independent women.
Includes index.
1. Pym, Barbara—Criticism and interpretation.
2. Sex role in literature.   3. Women in literature.
I. Janice Rossen
PR6066.Y58Z7   1988   823'.914   88–699
ISBN 0–312–02042–2 (St. Martin's Press)

1 2 3 4 5 92 91 90 89 88

For Philip Larkin (*In Memoriam*)
and Lord David Cecil

Contents

Preface

The animated discussion of Barbara Pym's novels which began in full force with the 'rediscovery' of her work in 1977 seemed at first astonishing for its enthusiasm; roughly a decade later, it continues to be remarkable for its thoughtfulness, breadth and diversity. The essays in this collection continue the study of Pym's life as it relates to her fiction, and of the significance of her work in the context of the English literary heritage and recent developments in critical thinking.

The volume is primarily scholarly in emphasis, and analyses Pym's literary achievement through various perspectives, taking biographical, historical and feminist approaches. It also pays tribute to the author herself, including reminiscences from some of Pym's long-time friends and admirers. The aim of the authors throughout the collection has been to elucidate Pym's novels in a way which not only defines how they are constructed, but why they delight, instruct and (in Pym's own words) 'comfort'—or, conversely, cause acute discomfort in the reader. Like her fiction as a whole, the effect of Barbara Pym's 'subtext' should not be underrated. Her particular gift is comedy, and though she remains kindly and genial, her satire can be shrewd and occasionally bitter as well.

To consider how Pym achieved her stylistic effects or how she (almost unaccountably) became a distinguished novelist is to further appreciate her work. The frivolity and modest good humour which was an essential part of her character finds expression in her novels; the darkness of a life filled with disappointments and frustrations appears there as well. Wit and graciousness marked her novelistic voice, even as she used

it to describe the experience of acute suffering. Irony is a fine
thing in itself, but it is all the more so when it makes us laugh.

Janice Rossen
Chapman College

Notes on the Contributors

Barbara Bowman is Associate Professor of English and Chair of the English Department at Illinois Wesleyan University. She has published a monograph on Nathaniel Hawthorne's short fiction and articles on the Gothic novel and film. She is currently completing a study of film space in American films of the 1930s and 1940s.

Charles Burkhart is Professor of English at Temple University. His most recent book is *The Pleasure of Miss Pym*.

Laura L. Doan is Assistant Professor of English and Humanities at Stetson University. She is the editor of *Old Maids and Excellent Women: The Spinster in the Twentieth-Century Novel*, a collection of essays that includes her article on Pym's treatment of the single woman, 'Pym's Problem: The Textual Definition of Self as Spinster'. Her research focuses on postwar British literature and culture.

Barbara Everett is a Senior Research Fellow of Somerville College and a lecturer at the University of Oxford. She has published widely on English literature. Her most recent book is *Poets in Their Time: Essays on English Poetry from Donne to Larkin*.

Jan Fergus is Associate Professor of English at Lehigh University. She has published *Jane Austen and the Didactic Novel* and is bringing out *Jane Austen: The Literary Career*. She is currently engaged in a study of the reading public in eighteenth-century England.

Hazel Holt worked for twenty-five years with Barbara Pym at the International African Institute. As Barbara Pym's literary executor she has prepared for the press the typescripts of *An Unsuitable Attachment* (1982), *Crampton Hodnet* (1985), *An Academic Question* (1986) and *Civil to Strangers and Other Stories* (1987). She has edited, with Hilary Pym, Barbara Pym's letters and diaries, published as *A Very Private Eye* (1984). She is currently working on the official biography.

Janice Rossen is Assistant Professor of English at Chapman College. She is the author of *The World of Barbara Pym* and is currently completing a book on Philip Larkin and a study of twentieth-century academic satire.

Robert Smith was educated at Oxford and has spent many years in West Africa, finally as Professor of History at the University of Ibadan in Nigeria. He is now retired, living near London. His correspondence with Barbara Pym is lodged in the Bodleian Library.

Roger Till is a former Senior Staff Tutor in the University of Durham Department of Extra-Mural Studies. He has contributed humorous verse to a number of journals and anthologies. His wife, Margaret Till, is an artist. Their correspondence with Barbara Pym is lodged in the Bodleian Library.

Anne M. Wyatt-Brown is a lecturer in linguistics at the University of Florida, Gainesville. She has published articles on E.M. Forster, Barbara Pym and in the field of gerontology. She is currently finishing a study of Barbara Pym's creative process.

Acknowledgements

The contributors would like to thank the Estate of Barbara Pym, Jonathan Cape Ltd and E.P. Dutton Inc. for permission to quote from *Some Tame Gazelle, Excellent Women, Jane and Prudence, Less than Angels, A Glass of Blessings* and *No Fond Return of Love*; and to the Estate of Barbara Pym, Macmillan London Ltd and E.P. Dutton Inc. for giving permission to quote from *An Unsuitable Attachment, Quartet in Autumn, The Sweet Dove Died, A Few Green Leaves, Crampton Hodnet, An Academic Question* and *A Very Private Eye: An Autobiography in Diaries and Letters*. Thanks are due to *London Review of Books* for permission to reprint Barbara Everett's essay. The contributors are also very grateful to Hilary Pym and Hazel Holt, as well as to the Bodleian Library, Oxford, for permission to quote from the collection of Pym's private papers.

The editor would like to thank Terri Joseph, who suggested the idea of the volume, and also Dale Salwak, Jean Wyatt, John Augustine and Stanley Porter, who gave invaluable advice on completing it. Kathryn McMillan undertook several Arduous and Thankless Tasks in preparing the manuscript for publication, and William Rossen was (as always) a Tower of Strength (a Real Tower).

List of Abbreviations

Page numbers are noted in brackets within the text. Dutton editions of Pym's novels are referred to throughout, using the following abbreviations:

STG   *Some Tame Gazelle* (1950, rpt 1983)
EW   *Excellent Women* (1952, rpt 1978)
JP   *Jane and Prudence* (1953, rpt 1981)
LTA   *Less than Angels* (1955, rpt 1980)
GB   *A Glass of Blessings* (1958, rpt 1980)
NFR   *No Fond Return of Love* (1961, rpt 1982)
QA   *Quartet in Autumn* (1977, rpt 1978)
SDD   *The Sweet Dove Died* (1978, rpt 1979)
FGL   *A Few Green Leaves* (1980)
UA   *An Unsuitable Attachment* (1982)
VPE   *A Very Private Eye: An Autobiography in Diaries and Letters* (1984)
CH   *Crampton Hodnet* (1985)
AQ   *An Academic Question* (1986)

References to Pym's private papers are cited according to manuscript and folio numbers, also within brackets in the text. The papers are lodged in the Bodleian Library, Oxford.

Introduction

JANICE ROSSEN

The question 'Who is Barbara Pym?' may soon come to be replaced by the question 'Why go *on* about Barbara Pym?' Her novels having been discovered, or 'rediscovered' through Philip Larkin and Lord David Cecil in 1977, some critics have asked if they might not be allowed to lapse back into the convenient category of simply a 'good read', or 'good books for a bad day?'[1] Various answers might be broached, and any tentative responses must take account of some peculiar circumstances. First of all, it is possible that Pym suffers mildly in academic circles because she is suspiciously popular with the general reader. Paperback editions of Pym's novels seem to be readily available in one's local bookstore in the way one's favourite books seldom are. Surprisingly, a volume of extracts from her private papers, *A Very Private Eye: An Autobiography in Diaries and Letters* (1984), spent a modest few weeks on the best-seller list in the United States. It can be difficult to appreciate Pym because of the the prosaic nature of her novels; her forte is understatement and reserve. She writes witty, provincial comedies of manners about educated, upper-middle-class English men and women on 'the dustier fringes of the academic world' or in the Anglican church (*NFR*, 13). Her settings rarely vary from suburban London or small villages. Her characters are the stuff of stock English fiction: spinsters, curates, dons, vicars' wives and elderly dowagers. Yet she transforms a world of modest proportions into a stage for piercing psychological analysis and keen social commentary. Above all, she writes hugely funny books.

Pym is an anachronistic writer in her penchant for tradition-

1

al novelistic subjects and form, and this suggests intriguing connections with her Victorian predecessors. Her place in contemporary British literature has been difficult to establish in part because it has been overshadowed by the debate about whom she most resembles in the past: Austen, Trollope, C.M. Yonge, Brontë and numerous others have all been suggested as influences on Pym's writing.[2] Further, her insight remains shrewd yet subtle. She was a feminist writer in the 1950s before feminism became fashionable. And she was a finely malicious satirist in the tradition of Huxley, Waugh and Amis, when these authors were writing increasingly raucous and mordant novels, in contrast to her own understated books. Also problematic to Pym's evolving literary reputation is the posthumous publication of work which is not her best.[3]

Finally, an enormous amount of scholarship discussing Pym's work seems to have sprung into being almost instantaneously—and in staggering quantity. Such an influx of commentary might well be expected, given Pym's erratic publishing history. The author was relatively unknown until quite late in her life (1913–80), at which point her *oeuvre* was nearly complete and offered an inviting cache of material for study. Still, such widespread interest can seem rash or ill-considered. The question of her reputation debated by scholars continues to be problematic, as the natural tendency to overpraise her work initially has led to a predictable reaction against inflated judgements. The issue has crystallized into an outright battle over Pym's literary reputation. A.S. Byatt, herself a very fine novelist, asked quite rightly in a *Times Literary Supplement* review, 'Why, therefore, this sudden blossoming of critical attention to Pym's *oeuvre*? . . . why the PhD dissertations, the academic conferences, *La Narrativa di Barbara Pym*, "Text and Sub-text in the Novels of Barbara Pym," etc.?'[4] Following the decade during which these issues have surfaced and begun to be debated, it seems a good time to re-examine the nature of Pym's accomplishments and the usefulness of further comment on her work. Is there, in fact, anything more to be said?

The following essays make an excellent case for continuing the discussion—and it suggests that some fascinating and intriguing discoveries can result from further study of Pym's life and work. Not only is this material relevant to our understanding of Pym and her contemporary novelists, but it is extremely interesting. In addition, these essays touch on broader critical issues relating to the creative process, literary influence, fictional subversive subtext and other problems of narration. They suggest several reasons why we read, and continue to read, Pym: because of her wit, her inventiveness and flights of fancy; because of her ingenious use of nineteenth-century fictional material; because of her ability to talk about the plight of the oppressed, even to identify them in unexpected places; and ultimately because she deals with the compelling theme of crushing disappointment. Her marginalized social groups might be bachelors and spinsters, and her primary example of disappointment might be unrequited love, but the issues she addresses are none the less compelling.

This volume falls into four main divisions, each of which addresses a particular aspect of Pym's life and work. The first part, 'The Creative Process', generally considers her novels in biographical context, asking why she wrote, how her imagination developed and what personal experiences might have shaped the novels. The second part, 'New Approaches', discusses Pym's attitude toward men, specifically the figures of both bachelors and homosexuals. It includes essays which primarily, though not exclusively, take a feminist perspective. The third part, 'Literary Heritage', studies covert and hidden allusions in Pym's fiction, focusing on the strong influence which Austen and Brontë have exerted on her work. The final section, 'Reminiscences', includes personal recollections from people who knew the author.

Within the 'Creative Process' section of the book, Barbara Everett begins the collection in 'The Pleasures of Poverty' with her consideration of Pym's creative process as it relates to her literary career. The essay traces through Pym's diaries, and the effects of disastrous love affairs, Pym's startling evolution into a 'Novelist'. This transformation begins to occur when an off-key obliquity in speaking of serious matters—especially emotional ones—becomes intrinsic to Pym's style. Her novels can be characterized as romantic anti-romances, which contain irony and scepticism. Anne M. Wyatt-Brown undertakes an extensive biographical and critical analysis of Pym's

creative process in 'Ellipsis, Eccentricity and Evasion in the
Diaries of Barbara Pym'. Discussing Pym's childhood at
length, Wyatt-Brown draws on a close reading of Pym's
private papers in the Bodleian Library and on several personal
interviews with Hilary Walton and Hazel Holt. The essay
suggests that patterns set in Pym's childhood, as well as
parental role models, account for much of her narrative
strategies in her mature fiction. Ellipses and evasion in the
author's diaries resulted indirectly in repetitious patterns in
her novels. Of particular interest is Wyatt-Brown's discussion
of Pym's relationship with Rupert Gleadow, her first serious
suitor at Oxford University, and the influence of Aldous
Huxley on her novels. In 'The Home Front: Barbara Pym's
Years in Oswestry', Hazel Holt, Pym's literary executor and
official biographer, gives us several extracts from Pym's unpublished writings during her years at home with her parents
in Oswestry. This period between taking her degree at Oxford
and the beginning of the war proved to be both frustrating, as
Pym could not find a publisher at the time, and ultimately
fruitful, as the writing she completed during these years
proved a catalyst for her mature fiction to follow.

Laura L. Doan examines the single man as a force in Pym's
work in 'Text and the Single Man: The Bachelor in Pym's
Dual-Voiced Narrative'. Critics have often considered the
figure of the spinster in Pym's fictional world, but the bachelor
plays a particularly important role within the world of the
novels. Curiously, the single man's relative freedom from
social ties makes him increasingly self-absorbed and
egotistical—a fact which leads ultimately to isolation and
eccentricity. Doan examines the bachelor's capacity to disrupt
the dual-voiced narration of the novels, thus showing how
Pym's sexual ideology informs her narrative structure. In
'Barbara Pym's Subversive Subtext: Private Irony and Shared
Detachment', Barbara Bowman discusses recurrent linguistic
patterns in the way Pym's narrators and heroines think and
speak. Their subversiveness—which occurs in an inner,
private space—allows them to challenge the complacency of
the characters around them who conform to the dominant
culture. Charles Burkhart's 'Glamourous Acolytes: Homosexuality in Pym's World' considers the role of the homosex-

ual male in Pym's novels. In a world dominated by boorish and avaricious 'straight' men, the homosexual can offer Pym's heroines solace, though it is only a partial solution to their loneliness.

The two following essays deal specifically with literary influences on Pym's work. In 'A Glass of Blessings, Emma and Barbara Pym's Art of Allusion', Jan Fergus discusses Pym's characters' allusions to literary works, which reflect their search—either comic, poignant or ambiguous—for significant expression or for consolation. Fergus demonstrates how in A Glass of Blessings covert allusions to Austen's Emma partially control the novel's form and content. 'On Not Being Jane Eyre: The Romantic Heroine in Barbara Pym's Novels' traces the influence of Brontë's Jane Eyre on Pym's work. In many different instances she can be seen to be writing against this romantic tradition. The essay discusses the figure of the romantic heroine in Pym's novels, and her characters' simultaneous relief yet disappointment that they are 'not at all like Jane Eyre' (EW, 7). The final part, 'Reminiscences', focuses on the author herself. In a more personal vein, Robert Smith offers 'Remembering Barbara Pym', recalling lunches and outings with the novelist throughout a friendship that lasted some thirty years. The essay concludes with comments on Pym's favourite authors, noting in particular her fondness for Denton Welch. In 'Coincidence in a Bookshop', Roger Till describes his own and his wife's fondness for Pym's novels during her years of literary eclipse, and their eventual meeting with her. Both Robert Smith and the Tills draw on their extensive correspondence with Barbara Pym, now lodged in the Bodleian Library.

The questions which these writers address in the essays which follow range from a consideration of how (and why) Pym became a novelist, to how she reworked earlier literary material, to more specific queries. What was she like as a person? What did she think about men? Was she a covert feminist? In speculating on possible answers, we offer them in the conviction that Pym was indeed a fine novelist, as well as a unique and extraordinary woman.

Notes

1. The 'rediscovery' of Pym's work was precipitated by a mock survey in the *Times Literary Supplement* (Jan. 1977), where both Philip Larkin and Lord David Cecil proclaimed Pym's novels to be 'underrated'. This in turn led to wide critical and popular acclaim. Robert Smith, in the first essay published on her work, emphasized their charm and characterized her novels as 'good books for a bad day' (Robert Smith, 'How Pleasant to Know Miss Pym', *Ariel: A Review of International English Literature* 2 [Oct. 1971]: 63).
2. It is possible that early reviewers of Pym's work tended to invoke the name of Jane Austen and other masters of the craft simply in order to convince the public to begin to read Pym's novels. She is indeed often compared to much greater writers than herself, which ironically can tend to devalue her work to readers who approach it with different expectations. Austen she is not; nor Chekhov nor Tolstoy. Still, as several essays in this collection point out, she was both influenced by a distinctive English literary tradition (including Huxley, Charlotte Brontë, Denton Welch and others) and the creator of her own distinctive style. Most importantly, although the attempt to place Pym in literary context is worthwhile, to insist that placing her means to define her can be reductive.
3. Posthumous publication of an author's lesser works is, of course, not unique to Barbara Pym. It has here, perhaps, particular consequences for her reputation since 'discovery' of her work is so recent, and its place in literary context often tends to be debated on the merits of newly issued novels. One review of *An Academic Question* raises the issue of the novel's value and decides in favour of the book: 'There is no clear way of deciding about the wisdom and propriety of posthumous publications, but in this case I agree, with mild ambivalence, that the decision to publish was correct. The story is complete, although it does not come to us directly from its author's hand'. The reviewer concludes that the novel 'harmonizes with the larger body of work, even if it is a little rough-edged at moments.' (Edmund Fuller, 'Tale No. 12: Essentially Pym', review of *An Academic Question*, in *Wall Street Journal*, 9 September 1986). A.S. Byatt's assessment of the novel in the *Times Literary Supplement* (she sees it as 'thin and unappealing') strikes me as a much more convincing judgement. Even so, the larger body of Pym's work remains, I think, rich and compelling—and can be seen as such in light of this additional manuscript.
4. A.S. Byatt, 'Marginal Lives', *TLS*, 8 August 1986, p. 862.

PART ONE: THE CREATIVE PROCESS

Barbara Pym is eminently a self-made novelist. Though a few of her friends were writers, she did not belong to any well-defined literary group; nor did early publishing success encourage her to persevere in writing. In fact, it is difficult to understand how—from such a relatively unpromising start—she came to be a distinguished novelist. She clearly perceived herself to be a budding author during her days at Oxford University (1931–4), when she first began writing *Some Tame Gazelle*. Yet the fact that she did not succeed in publishing this first novel until several years later (1950) reflects a long period of apprenticeship. In part, she achieved the aim of becoming a novelist through practice, as evidenced by the sheer number of manuscript drafts she composed during the 1930s and 1940s. Yet she also seems to have developed a new and cogent way of transmuting her experience into fiction. The following essays, generally taking a biographical approach to Pym's work, address the evolution of her talent as a writer, with special attention to her early years as a novelist just after going down from Oxford University, when she lived at home with her parents in Oswestry. These essays suggest various perspectives on Pym's creative process and the shaping of her novelistic imagination.

Chapter 1

The Pleasures of Poverty

BARBARA EVERETT

The Barbara Pym story is possibly better-known than any of her novels, widely though these are now read. During the decade after 1950 she brought out half a dozen books, which were well received and found a steady if small reading public. But in 1963 her publisher, Cape, turned down her new novel, *An Unsuitable Attachment*, and she stayed unpublished until 1977. In that year, two contributors to a *Times Literary Supplement (TLS)* survey, Philip Larkin and Lord David Cecil, spoke so highly of her work as to effect a change in this situation. Three more novels by Barbara Pym were published, this time by Macmillan, who finally added to them in 1982— two years after the writer had herself died—the book originally rejected by Cape. Meanwhile, notice excited by the *TLS* survey of 1977 created new readers and admirers of Barbara Pym, and her reputation continues to grow.

There are different ways of interpreting this history. Accidents do happen, and people do ' "[fall] through the net" ' (the phrase used ironically in Barbara Pym's own *Quartet in Autumn* [*QA*, 21]). Those who are sceptical of this may prefer another kind of explanation, more sociological or even political. It would involve some comment on the adequacy or otherwise of publishers' readers, and on the principles or otherwise of publishers themselves, and on the reality or otherwise of market demand. A reading public may have as much to do with publicity as with reading. It is perhaps partly in deference to this belief, and to help prevent Barbara Pym's 'image' from being lost again to public view, that her friend and literary executor Hazel Holt, and her sister Hilary Pym, put together from the writer's journals and letters what they call an 'Autobiography', *A Very Private Eye*. Its very title suggests a joky apologetic gesture towards what is seen as the problem of being a private writer needing a public reputation.

This interpretation too leaves room for doubts. If Barbara Pym's misfortunes were simply the product of her lack of public note, her career a kind of fault in the whole public system of communications, they would have come to an end with her 'rediscovery'. But they didn't. In fact, even her own too-early death didn't see an end to them. Her obituary in *The Times*, composed one can only imagine by some loyal friend, filled much of its space with an indignant dismissal of the notion that this dead writer might be said to approach the standard of Jane Austen. When *An Unsuitable Attachment*, posthumously published, was reviewed in the *London Review of Books*, Marilyn Butler devoted her analysis to the thesis that the novelist was not the anti-feminist old-men's-darling that she pretended to be, but was really, under the influence of modern anthropology, purposively producing 'Functionalist' or essentially external accounts of her main subject through-out, the condition of the contemporary Church of England. I find it hard to think that this reading improves on what it is presumably directed against: sentimental absorption of Barbara Pym's work into the world of the genteel novelette. Thus Macmillan have sold her novels in dust-jackets whose blurbs offer the quietly formidable and truthful *Jane and Prudence* as an 'engaging world . . . in which pale young curates send hearts aflutter'; and the desolating, entirely contemporary village of *A Few Green Leaves* similarly appears as 'the picture of life in a town forgotten by time'.

It would be absurd to make Barbara Pym's ten novels—light, dry and unpretentious as they are—sound obscure or difficult. Their salient qualities can be caught, or at least intimated, in a brief essay. There is really nothing to add, for instance, to the finely economical yet comprehensive five pages on 'The World of Barbara Pym' which Philip Larkin devoted to the first six novels published, and reprints in his *Required Writing*; and there is an equally penetrating and suggestive and even briefer account of these earlier novels in Karl Miller's review of *Jane and Prudence* in the *London*

Review of Books. Even such admirable essays as these have, however, one curious limitation. They don't quite suggest a writer who has such difficulties as met Barbara Pym during her literary career, and even less of course do they explain these difficulties.

Conversely, it seems interesting that both her obituarist and the *London Review of Books* reviewer of the rejected novel give the same impression of going wide of the mark, despite the apparent distance between the presumed sympathy of the first and the open antipathy of the second. Both are perhaps reflecting some real uncertainty presented by their subject, some essential elusiveness and problematical quality. It seems only just to say that if the obituary sounds uncharitable, this may be an effect of a genuine attempt to come to terms with an underlying principle of Barbara Pym's work, the determined 'smallness' of her fictions; and the resulting problem of *status* is equalled by the problem of *kind* that meets the brisk unadmiring inquiry of the academic eager to categorize. Both suggest the possibility of a writer less lucidly simple than the best criticism can make her sound.

A great part of the interest of *A Very Private Eye* is that it supports this impression. The book does this, first, by mere information that extends what we already know of Barbara Pym's publishing history. From the writing point of view hers was a hard-knock life from beginning to end; *not* getting published was almost more intrinsic to her career than its opposite. When her first novel, *Some Tame Gazelle*, came out in 1950, Barbara Pym was 37; the 'Autobiography' reveals that this first book had then been twice revised and many times rejected since she first wrote it in 1934 and 1935, when she herself was only 21 or 22. Even during the decade after she had achieved publication, problems remained. In a letter written to her close friend Bob Smith, Barbara Pym lightly passes on the information from Cape that 'eight Americans and ten Continental publishers saw and "declined" . . . *Excellent Women* and they are still plodding on with [*Jane and Prudence*]' (*VPE*, 191); and this is in 1954, when she might have been assumed to be well and truly launched. These misfortunes may, again, be wholly externalized; we could say that such publishers as found Barbara Pym's novels not right for the mood of the

1960s, are supported by those publishers who thought them not right, either, for the 1950s, 1940s or 1930s, and above all by those publishers outside the British Isles who thought them not right for any decade. But *A Very Private Eye* gives some suggestion that someone more considerable found Barbara Pym's work difficult or problematic: and that was the writer herself. Apart from providing information, the 'Autobiography' in itself helps to show that, like many true artists and unlike many mere entertainers (though she was both, and both with distinction), she may have found it hard not only to perfect her essential gift but even to articulate it.

This is suggested by the particular character of the 'Autobiography' as a whole, and more especially by the way in which the writer presents herself in it. Though from time to time in the journals she directly addresses a 'Reader' whom she imagines absorbed in the text, there is nothing like an appropriate shaping in the materials, which merely follow a loose chronological sequence. The major events of Barbara Pym's life were probably the acceptance of her first novel in 1950, the rejection of her seventh in 1963, and her 'rediscovery' in 1977. Appropriately, the latter or post-1950 part of the book is in the nature of excerpts from a novelist's working notebooks, which she kept up even through her long period of enforced silence. Interspersed with these are letters to three friends, pleasant but neither long nor introspective, many indeed as concerned with the fate of her writing as her own essential modesty permitted. The background to this part of her life is London, where she set up house with her sister and took up her first full-time professional employment, helping to edit an anthropological journal: ill-health, however, forced her to retire early, at 60, to a small house—again shared with her sister—in an Oxfordshire village, where she died six or seven years later. It is in the earlier or pre-1950 parts of *A Very Private Eye* that we find 'Autobiography' in a perhaps more substantial and revealing sense. Here we meet the 20-year-old Barbara Pym at Oxford in the early 1930s (like many others, she found it hard to leave, and lingered on); then on visits home to Shropshire, briefly to Germany, and—more briefly still—to Poland (she travelled more widely than the novels suggest, and after the war was fairly often in Greece); then from 1939 on, in war-work with the censorship in Bristol, until to escape from an unhappy love-affair she joined the Wrens and spent the rest of the war with them in Italy.

These early journals in particular leave a reader responding somewhat ambiguously to Pym's character. We don't, that is to say, really meet 'Barbara Pym' in these early journals at all, given that the reader's Barbara Pym must be the writer of the novels—must be some kind of writer, at least. And it seems doubtful if the author of these early journals can write at all. Indeed, not many readers of these diaries could predict that she ever would be able to, despite the fact that at 20 she 'Bought a lovely fat book at Blackwell's to write my novel in' (*VPE*, 20). This work must have turned out to be the first version of *Some Tame Gazelle*, which was, alone of all her novels, taken from life, in the sense of being a *roman-à-clef*. It tells the story of her great unreciprocated passion for another undergraduate, 'Henry', in the form of a long-enduring tenderness felt by a 50-year-old maiden lady for a married and unlovable Archdeacon. The very ability so to rework her own situation suggests a remarkable detachment, humour and originality— all in all, a literary power well outside anything shown in these journals from the time. Perhaps Barbara Pym merely lacked the right egoism to make a good diarist. The first draft of the novel, if published, would throw light on this, but it seems to me probable that it would be very different from the final version.

For *A Very Private Eye* suggests a good deal about the whole process by which Barbara Pym became a writer, and seems to make it plain that that process couldn't have been speeded up; the novels appearing after 1950 were genuinely the product of the life. The younger Barbara Pym's great problem was that of not knowing, in any very clear sense, 'who she was'; and in so far as she did know who she wanted to be, she didn't really (despite the 'fat book') want to be a writer. When she got to Oxford she promptly rechristened herself 'Sandra' (and embroidered the name all over her cushions). Sandra's literary style is embroidered all over the journal too: its first entry reads: '*15 January* [1932]. A new term in a new year—a golden opportunity to get a peer's heir—a worthy theological student —or to change entirely! But Oxford really is intoxicating'

(*VPE*, 13). In so far as the writer of these early journals has any kind of coherent style or voice, she seems a not unlikeable, very commonplace, big, bonny, bouncing girl, whose attention is mesmerized by the conventional: her love of the sheerly social sphere of existence making all the more touchingly noticeable her great lack of any appropriate social mastery of utterance. Her dashing derivative manner is hardly more than the function of a permanent hopeful high self-consciousness. But its falsity, though innocent, is unpromising: so much so that there is a curiously strong relief when at moments the Sandra style breaks down, and another voice—though still not the novelist's—makes itself heard. Invariably this is 'the true voice of feeling'. Thus, in the late summer of 1936, the young Barbara Pym says in a letter to 'Henry', with a kind of ruthless truthful desolation, 'I don't believe letters should be written like this, especially from people like me to people like you. It would be better if I could write you a poem' (*VPE*, 61).

It is part of the later novelist's admirable naturalness and good sense never to seem to come near to valuing art over life. Consonantly, the younger Barbara Pym wanted only two things: she wanted love and marriage. These early journals are largely an account of her frequently unhappy and always fruitless quest for both. There are quite a number of affairs, and a lot of romantic agony: 'at lunch-time when I was alone, I *howled*'—so she writes in March 1943, while trying to recover from the second great love of her life; and, despite all the continual business of 'being drearily splendid', life during the preceding decade was often a matter of 'breaking down for a minute' and '*howling*' (*VPE*, 116–17). Through the 1930s and 1940s the diarist downrightly hopes for marriage, or at least love ('No words will describe this wonderful nebulous lover that may one day materialize': *VPE*, 126). The journals reiterate, painfully and for some years almost obsessively, the wish not to be, nor to be seen as, what she in fact anxiously-too-early sees herself as being: 'the bewildered English spinster, now rather gaunt and toothy, but with a mild, sweet expression' (*VPE*, 122). This mocking, harping self-characterization seems to reflect two sides of the writer's nature. One is a frank response to the socially *convenable*, a humane and simple wish to do what other people do, to go 'the way of the world'. The other is a deep source of much more inward idealism.

Often in the earlier journals these opposed feelings come together, when larger issues have failed her, in a fascinated interest in clothes. The still-unpublished novelist, working with the Censorship in Bristol and trying to forget an (on her side) painfully intense love-affair, writes:

> *Thursday 15 April* [1943]. I went to Woolworth's in the lunch hour and bought various beauty aids—also looked longingly at ginghams and cherry-red linen in Jolly's window. Oh, but the sun was shining, and in the afternoon a bird sang so that it could be heard even among the censors. (*VPE*, 124)

Underlying the women's magazinish simplicities of 'Woolworth's' and 'beauty aids' and 'ginghams' and 'cherry-red linen' is a simplicity of natural emotion that extends itself in the last sentence towards a hint of transcendental idealism. A new heaven and a new earth are hard to come by; but a new dress may be made in an afternoon. At this point Barbara Pym begins to be recognizable as an artist: by the way in which all that is pleasantly unpretentious in her social world fuses with a more personal vision of love and the English Church. In however muted and reticent a form, such romanticism was the mainspring of her character, and from it comes that inwardness which makes the early journals, with their central 'pursuit of love', so frequently touching. At the same time they are often strikingly inarticulate.

While she was still an undergraduate, Barbara Pym went to Stratford to see *Romeo and Juliet*, and 'it was all terribly tragic—both Romeo and Juliet were intensely passionate, especially Romeo'. For ten years after this, the journals are the record of an 'intensely passionate' and perhaps even slightly tragic young woman. And yet they hardly communicate much of it directly, just as the diarist presumably responded to but can say little about Shakespeare's young lovers. Romanticism both powers and silences her. It is all the more remarkable, therefore, when—sometime around 1950, where the section called by the editors 'The Novelist' begins (the journals are thin for half a dozen years before)—a page is turned and the new working-notebook is recognizable as true Barbara Pym.

Thirty years later, the last sentence of her last novel, *A Few Green Leaves*, would leave its heroine reflecting in understatement and in the conditional tense, envisaging not only the writing of a novel but the possibility of 'a love affair which need not necessarily be an unhappy one' (*FGL*, 250). And this offhand, off-key obliquity in speaking of serious matters, especially matters of feeling, is here for the first time intrinsic to the novelist's style. In the second half of the journals it is this note of impassive and ironic observation that replaces the earlier clamorous but ineffective appeal. Above all, the new voice is a style of self-containment.

In 1936 Barbara Pym had written in her diary, 'I often think Henry is never so nice as when he's standing at the door of the flat saying good-bye' (*VPE*, 58). 'Saying good-bye' is of course in itself a pure and classic Romantic experience (in Keats it is Joy himself who has his hand ever at his lips). The individual quality of Barbara Pym's writing in the novels is to seem perpetually caught in a kind of smiling farewell to romanticism itself. The later phase of the journals occasionally permits a reader to see how thoroughly her idealism has been transformed by that dry clarity of mind that haunts her fiction— what she calls, in a letter to Philip Larkin later again, 'a novelist's cruelly dispassionate eye'. The continued solitariness of her life, despite her work, her social instincts, and her capacity for strong emotion, has given her a habit of independence; it has also left her free to take stock of and to analyse the powerful romantic imagination which has formed the inner history of her first thirty years. Certainly the later diaries, like the painful and dark novels published late in her career, have a clear understanding of the degree to which intense romantic feeling may be as much a creation of the self as a recognition of the other: as solitary in reality as it is in wish social.

In March 1962 (before the rejection of *An Unsuitable Attachment*, and before she had met the much younger and presumably homosexual 'Richard', who was her last love, and who pained her so much by withdrawing), she describes in her journal how she had bought a damaged little china bowl with a lemon and leaves painted inside it, and liked it so much as to wonder 'if I am getting to the stage when objects could please more than people'. She follows this with a bleak project for a story:

A woman living in the country who has had a hopeless love for a
man (wife still living perhaps or religious scruples), then, when he
is free she finds that after all he means nothing to her—is this the
reward of virtue, this nothingness? (*VPE*, 206)

The word 'nothing' comes to have a certain potency in Barbara
Pym's later journals. In September 1964, when she was happiest with 'Richard', an idea for her novel *The Sweet Dove
Died* came to her as: 'She (Leonora) thinks perhaps this is the
kind of love I've always wanted because absolutely *nothing*
can be done about it!' (*VPE*, 229). Then, after the break, she
writes in February 1967 to her friend Bob Smith about her
'total "failure" (if that's the word) with Richard. Trying to
understand people and leaving them alone and being "unselfish" and all *that* jazz has only the bleakest of rewards—
precisely nothing!' (*VPE*, 242).

An Unsuitable Attachment is a novel difficult to think about
clearly without knowing just how much of it survives from its
first pre-1963 version. The other three late novels, *The Sweet
Dove Died, Quartet in Autumn* and *A Few Green Leaves*, are
all very fine achievements; but they have, despite some surviving humour and tenderness, a considerable darkness within
them. It would be natural to see that darkness as at least in part
the result of Barbara Pym's hard fortunes in her publishing
career, cheerfully and stoically as they were borne. The journals show how much her romanticism, her sense of life as a
place of ideals, came as youth left her to depend on her pride in
literary creativity, and this was taken from her. So much seems
clearly true. But nothing in Barbara Pym's work appears
simply the effect of accident. The darkness of the last novels
has in fact its own continuity with what is romantic, what is
golden, in the first and happier comedies.

At the end of *Less than Angels*, there is a scene in which the
sad and tough women's-magazine-writing Catherine helps the
failed anthropologist Alaric to burn a professional lifetime's
notes on the bonfire in his back garden one Guy Fawke's night.
Later, watching them from an upstairs window next-door,
two kindly middle-aged female neighbours reflect, 'But oh
dear . . . if ever Catherine and Alaric should marry, what a
difficult and peculiar couple they would make!' (*LTA*, 256).

The romanticism of these early novels works just *because* they have respect for the 'difficult and peculiar'; they leave room for it, as in the insistent conditional tense of that closing sentence. Even the very first novel, the pastoral *Some Tame Gazelle*, is fully aware that pastoral is made for satire as much as for love; its English village has the formality (and surely had even in 1935) of something nostalgic, out-of-date, like its enchanted old-maid heroines; and even the title evokes an Elysium both tender and silly, both elegant and idiotic (as are the clergy cast as the story's love-objects, when they are not something worse). Its first paragraph has the heroine Belinda gazing thoughtfully at the long underwear left carelessly glimpsable by the curate beloved of her sister: 'Of course he might think it none of their business, as indeed it was not, but Belinda rather doubted whether he thought at all, if one were to judge by the quality of his first sermon.' Barbara Pym is always capable of a peculiarly comic because peculiarly hard but sideways kick—of an attack whose grace is its thorough inconsequentiality.

I mentioned earlier the anxiety expressed by the writer of Barbara Pym's obituary concerning any comparison with Jane Austen. It is true that the two artists are probably not much alike (though mere difference of scale does not forbid the comparison, since scale matters less with artists than their having achieved what is in their power to achieve). A better comparison, however, might be with a still greater writer, the creator of *Don Quixote*: for Barbara Pym's novels are surely in the same way romantic anti-romances. An entry in her journal during 1943 shows her taking interested notice of the English Quixotic tradition. Friends one day lent her Sterne's *Tristram Shandy*, which she found (though she never read it through, and was honest enough to say so) 'a nice, inconsequential sort of book—the sort of book one would like to have written—or might even one day write' (*VPE*, 123). In her novels Barbara Pym does aim at and achieve the beautifully 'inconsequential' in a number of different ways: lack of self-importance, a surprising gaiety and even a kind of mystery. But most of all her books possess 'inconsequentiality' in that aspect of them which caused most trouble in the market, and which she often refers to unhappily and anxiously in these diaries as her novels' 'mildness'.

Negatively, this is their reticence about sex and violence; but in more positive terms it is a question of her liking and seeing the necessity for a certain kind of smallness and randomness and unromantic ordinariness. All these are things which, perhaps, she came to prize in her own life as a larger 'Romance' ebbed from her, but which came in their turn to carry a kind of residue of ideality within themselves. A journal entry for May 1935 celebrates one of the rare occasions when 'Henry', feeling kind, took her out for the day on a jaunt: 'I meditated on how strange and wonderful it was to be in a train with Henry ... I suppose this is inevitable, as the most ordinary things done with someone one loves are full of new significance that they never have otherwise' (*VPE*, 50). It is this 'new significance' which got into Barbara Pym's books twenty years after the journal entry, and in them makes things of an unromantic ordinariness seem perhaps not so ordinary or so unromantic after all. Always these are what Charles Lamb called 'the Pleasures of Poverty', perceptions around which lingers a certain tough irony or scepticism. Thus, for instance, in *Jane and Prudence*, an unhappy rather cross middle-aged office-worker on the very fringes of the action happens to use a card-catalogue, and suddenly (brilliantly) turns into a comic artist rather like Barbara Pym herself: 'Miss Clothier drew a small card-index towards her and began moving the cards here and there with her fingers, as if she were coaxing music from some delicate instrument' (*JP*, 36).

Once one starts in this way to remember instances of Barbara Pym's ironic romanticism from the novels, there is (to use one of her own favourite phrases) 'such richness' as to make choice difficult. I want to mention one thing only which seems to me to indicate how much these wholly unpretentious fictions are at the same time something like an original prose *poésie de départs* ('I often think Henry is never so nice as when he's standing at the door of the flat saying good-bye'). Only two of her novels, the first and the last, are in their very different ways 'pastoral' in the sense of being set in villages. The others all take place chiefly in London and its suburbs—those least 'romantic' of all localities. It is curious how little evocative *A Very Private Eye* is in its sense of time and

place—how rarely Barbara Pym gives any glimpse, for instance, of Pimlico, Barnes and Queens Park, the London suburbs where the writer and her sister lived for most of her
writing life. It is the novels, *Less than Angels* and *No Fond
Return of Love* in particular, which create quite extraordin-
arily the precise 'feel', in depth, of a summer or autumn
evening in a south-west London suburb, at least as it was
twenty or thirty years ago. This haunting intensity is not
merely topographical. It derives from the way in which the
quiet self-respecting 'inconsequentiality' of a London suburb
has become an image of the possible truth and happiness that
can be found within such a place. The mere contingency of the
suburban renders up its rich possibilities: these tree-lined
streets and stolid houses have fascinating, even mysterious
lives opening out behind them—though lives subject to the
same dark laws of morality that (in *Quartet in Autumn*)
govern the fate of Marcia, Barbara Pym's most grotesque and
'romantic' character, dying alone in her suburban house.

As an artist of the suburban, Barbara Pym was not, in fact,
alone; she may even be seen as the last in a recognizable
English literary tradition. John Keats was the first great
English poet to grow up in the London suburbs, and—aided by
Leigh Hunt—to allow his work to speak for his true milieu.
Browning's aesthetic eccentricity might well be called sub-
urbanity, the decision to keep his independence by avoiding a
classic centre. And more recently, others besides Larkin and
Amis have created an alternative to Modernism by returning
to the parochial, the provincial and the suburban in tone and
ethos. Barbara Pym's 'private' eye was a style that caught the
realities of her social world with an intensity equivalent to that
of poetry.

Chapter 2

Ellipsis, Eccentricity and Evasion in the Diaries of Barbara Pym*

ANNE M. WYATT-BROWN

In July 1985, *Crampton Hodnet*, a recently exhumed manuscript from the Pym papers in the Bodleian Library, evoked a stern denunciation in the *London Review of Books*. The source of the reviewer's complaint was a letter by the author (written much earlier, during the composition of the novel) in which she had suggested that some of the incidents in the book 'might be a comfort to somebody' (*VPE*, 100). Nicholas Spice retorted, 'As well, it seems to me, call *The Rite of Spring* restful or *Guernica* entertaining as expect *Crampton Hodnet* to administer comfort.'[1] A month earlier, Anita Brookner, whose works have often been compared to Pym's, added some sharp comments of her own. In addition to accusing Pym of acting like a character from a soap opera, Brookner complained that the author had deliberately kept one of her characters, Barbara Bird, 'in her virginal state by some crude twists of plotting which makes one a little uneasy, as does the determined sexlessness of the authorial voice'.[2] What accounts for the intensity of these two reactions to Pym's novel? Nothing in the novels is as arresting as *Guernica*—nor even particularly sinister.

In fact, the surprising truth is that Pym was drawing on her own experience in creating both Miss Morrow and Miss Bird, two typical characters in the novel. If the world of *Crampton Hodnet* seems overpopulated by repressed spinsters, timid curates, pompous, middle-aged dons with redundant

* This chapter was partially funded by Sponsored Research, and also the English Department of the University of Florida, Gainesville.

21

manuscripts-in-progress, and aspiring young politicians who make unfaithful lovers, they all resemble people whom the author knew well. But since she actually shared a good many of the foibles of her characters, her narrative stance as a disinterested observer who dispassionately and ironically recounts their trivial adventures, is a literary construction. Its effect is to obscure the fact that the author poured her own feelings into the work. Pym wrote, according to her own statement, 'what pleases and amuses *me* in the hope that a few others will like it too' (MS PYM 96, f. 12). Not only do her own feelings and attitudes permeate the novels, but in some cases their plots contain restorative fantasies of enormous importance to her.[3] It is possible for the reader to be lulled into a false security by the cosy atmosphere of the novels. And yet her work has a satiric undercurrent. A sharp observation— what Philip Larkin called one of her torpedoes—periodically appears in order to devastate masculine, or occasionally feminine, pretensions (MS PYM 151, f. 115). No wonder unwary reviewers overreacted.

The mixed but often emotional reactions to Pym's work as a whole have ranged from intense distaste to great pleasure and delight.[4] The diversity of these responses testifies to the effect of the subtext of the novels on her audience. Pym's personality invades her literary world just as at Oxford she had once intruded on the world of Henry Harvey, an undergraduate whom she had fancied. In her writing, however, her eye for details and her acute sense of style distract attention from her personal involvement in the material. The critical outbursts regarding her writing represent in part an unconscious objection to or endorsement of the view of human relations her novels convey. Accordingly, because the reviewers rarely question the reasons for their individual reactions, critical opinion has generated much passion but has contributed relatively little to our understanding of Pym's work.

Now that it is possible to establish a connection between Pym's life and her writing from ample evidence in her diaries and journals, we can observe the circuitous route by which her romantic disasters, revised to her satisfaction, worked their way into her novels.[5] From her diaries, letters and journals one learns why she clung to the literary perspective she developed as quite a young girl, even though doing so left her vulnerable to social pressures, changing popular taste and the financial exigencies of the publishing world. Such knowledge adds greatly to our understanding of her creative process and helps to explain why she had so little control over the course of her career.

Aside from publishers' blurbs and occasional reviews, there was little information available about Pym during her lifetime. As a result, a few important misinterpretations have been popularly accepted. She has often been compared to Jane Austen, and once the news of her rejection by Cape became known, some suspected that she had been the innocent victim of her publisher's greed.[6] With the publication of extracts from Pym's private papers in 1984, however, it became apparent that Pym's own eccentricity had contributed its share to her personal tale of woe.[7] A Very Private Eye revealed that the author, whose novels were models of detached humour, had spent a good part of her life pursuing men who did not even pretend to be seriously interested in her. The editors, Hazel Holt and Hilary Pym Walton, staunchly published the journal entries and letters that described Pym's troubles, though they did not venture to interpret her behaviour or to assess her literary contributions.[8]

Pym's private papers reveal how distorted are these early assumptions about her life and work. Pym was not Jane Austen's inheritor, primarily because she lacked Austen's faith in the possibility of marriage.[9] Nor was she a martyr on the altar of feminism, although bias no doubt played its part. Establishing a corrective to these misconceptions is important because these overstatements of Pym's case have caused several English academics to react negatively to her books. For instance, when Marilyn Butler reviewed An Unsuitable Attachment, she expected to find a kindred spirit, or 'modern' Jane Austen. Instead, she was sorely disappointed.[10] In actual fact, Pym was a believer in romantic values, but a succession of unhappy love experiences taught her to trust to humour and detachment as a means of living with disappointment.

Although she was not especially a victim of her publishers' hostility to women writers, it is important to understand the forces that made Pym so vulnerable to their miscalculations.

Unfortunately, two factors coincided. First, she sometimes displayed a strange professional ineptness, the consequences of repeated rejections and a basic lack of confidence. Second, publishers in general, and Cape in particular, had uneasy finances and unaggressive marketing techniques.[11] After Jonathan Cape's death in 1960, new men took over the firm. The editor made responsible for Pym's work, Thomas Maschler, had never read one of Pym's novels as late as 1977.[12]

Fundamentally, Pym suffered from an extensive number of ironic twists and bitter disappointments throughout her career because she conceived of her literary stance in very narrow terms. Her role of diffident outsider who had little stake in the future was naturally antagonistic to the missionary impulse of the 1960s. But even in the 1930s, editors had deemed her work too old-fashioned to find a substantial market.[13]

As it turned out, the publishers were wrong. There was a constituency for her kind of novel, and in recent years her works have had enormous popularity. But to a large extent, Pym herself made no effort to reach that larger group. She had a natural affinity for the more eccentric, English reader; her fans were those whose refinements made them feel slightly out of place in the modern world.[14] According to their letters they were a small but articulate group of people much like herself, outsiders whose intelligence allowed them to observe accurately and acutely the social behaviour of people around them. Ironically, to please them and to gain the approval of this particular group, she willingly toned down her own sometimes flamboyant personality. A Navy friend from Pym's Second World War days in Italy wrote that he was startled by the unworldliness of Belinda in Some Tame Gazelle; he had expected a more up-to-date and sophisticated novel from the WRNS officer he had known (MS PYM 167, f. 28). Since Pym yearned for real popularity, which she might have achieved if she had allowed some outlet for her more earthy qualities, her avoidance of sexuality was a serious mistake.

As a result of Pym's self-imposed restrictions, during the 1950s when production costs rose, her royalties did not. Suddenly in 1954 she got an unexpected opportunity to better her position. Bad luck and attendant anxiety, however, caused her to refuse the proffered assistance. Graham Watson, a director of Curtis Brown, offered to find an American publisher for her novels (MS PYM 147, f. 175). Her initial reaction to his inquiry was positive. But when she learnt subsequently that Cape had unsuccessfully submitted *Excellent Women* and *Jane and Prudence* to nine and seven American firms respectively, she felt devastated by such massive rejection. Concluding that her books were unsuited to an American audience, she gave up her efforts to improve her status. As a result, Pym's never very robust confidence was badly shaken; she refused to discuss the matter in person and continued her downward course with Cape (MS PYM 147, f. 175–88). To have accepted Watson's help would have forced her to risk alienating the only publisher who had ever accepted her novels.

Unfortunately, it is now apparent that the change would have probably been worth the risk; not only were Cape's marketing techniques outmoded, but to have found a more enthusiastic supporter would have constituted a change that might well have counteracted the note of dull depression that had begun to creep into her work by *No Fond Return of Love*.[15] Sadly, it was easier for her to divert herself by keeping 'field notes' on her young male neighbours from October 1955 until June 1959 than to make plans that might have risked exacerbating her sense of humiliation if the strategy should fail (MS PYM 47–52).

The rest of Pym's publishing history illustrates the same combination of great personal effort and an undermining sense of pessimism about the worth of her novels. After Cape dropped her from their list, she sent out *An Unsuitable Attachment* and *The Sweet Dove Died* to virtually every London publisher. Again lack of confidence prevailed; some of her covering letters were models of self-effacement, and she found herself incapable of altering her techniques in order to write more popular fiction (MS PYM 165, f. 1). As a result, in 1977 she needed some miraculous intervention.[16]

Later events disproved the notion that her work had a limited appeal; otherwise there would be little reason to investigate her case. Her current popularity actually demonstrates how ephemeral taste can be. The multitude of reasons for the publishers' decision to refuse *An Unsuitable Attachment* would have seemed compelling as late as 1972, but in retrospect seems entirely to disregard the lasting qualities of Pym's work.[17] And indeed, changes in public taste might occur in future which would leave Pym once more on the periphery.

Since Pym's vulnerability to external forces probably results from her self-imposed restrictions about what constitutes proper material for a novel, it is important to turn to her childhood in order to understand the way in which she developed her artistic role. Certain conflicts from that early period were never resolved. Therefore she persisted in clinging to her youthful dreams and attitudes long after they had ceased to serve her, and even when it became apparent that such loyalty was costing her an audience.

In Pym's childhood, apparently her sexual and creative drives intertwined, leaving her at the mercy of a sometimes crippling sense of inhibition. Reconstructing the strands of her early life, however, is no easy matter. Little primary material has survived. The girlhood diaries that she reported rereading in 1933 are not among her papers. Furthermore, neither Barbara nor her sister Hilary Walton recall much about their childhood. Pym's fiction adds little to our knowledge of her past. She rarely wrote about children or childhood except for one novel about university life in the late 1960s, *An Academic Question* (1986). To compound the problem, Pym's characters seem also to have amnesia about their pasts. As a result, no corroborative evidence can be found there. Yet family life was very important to her, and the notebooks reveal that her pet formula for starting a new novel begins with a mother and two or three adult daughters who are living on their own. References to fathers occur infrequently, and these are chiefly in the prewar fragments. Aside from Nicholas Cleveland in *Jane and Prudence*, the fathers mentioned in Pym's fiction are safely dead, extremely pompous and silly, or clearly ridiculous, such as Francis Cleveland in *Crampton Hodnet* (1985; written in 1940).

What is known about Pym's early life, meagre as this information is, indicates the presence of some serious developmental issues. Because Barbara had a remarkable imagination and was, like many of her characters, 'observant beyond her emotional means', she had special needs that her parents were apparently unable to satisfy.[18] Exceptionally creative and sensitive children are not easy to rear, and her parents clearly did their best. Still, her father's gentle but ineffectual nature did not provide an adequate model of masculinity for her. Perhaps in reaction to, or in imitation of, her father's unassertive behaviour, Pym herself developed a life-long habit of overvaluing male strength and of mistaking aggression for evidence of male worth, an attitude which seems to account for her characteristic passivity in the face of unkind treatment.

As a child, she had very little direct experience with men. Women seemed to dominate the world in which she grew up, a fact which accounts in part for her preoccupation with the interaction of mothers and daughters, and the relative lack of importance of men in her fiction—except for vicars and politicians, who are institutionalized father figures. In her adult life, furthermore, she exhibited a desire to find strong mother-substitutes, an inclination which embroiled her in awkward rivalries at various points in her life. With those people who were willing to play a motherly role in her life, and in whom she confided, particularly Honor Wyatt and Robert Liddell, she behaved in a deeply ambivalent fashion. In both cases Barbara competed for the affection of a man in their lives—Honor's estranged husband, Gordon Glover, and Liddell's flatmate, Henry Harvey—but at the same time demanded their support and advice when the lovers treated her caddishly (MS PYM 102, 50; MS PYM 103, f. 10; VPE, 97, 122). Such childlike actions are reminiscent of oedipal behaviour, suggesting that Pym had not completely resolved some fundamental developmental conflicts of her youth.[19] Because she resisted the potential painfulness of introspection, at various points she felt irresistibly attracted by triangles that recreated familiar patterns she had long since forgotten.

Hilary Walton's recollections of their childhood in A Very Private Eye convey the distinct impression that Mrs Pym was the decisive force in the family. As it turns out, there were some practical reasons for her ascendancy. Hilary discovered, when she first saw her father's birth certificate, that he was illegitimate, a fact which Barbara had never learnt (VPE, 1). His grandparents had reared him, and he had no siblings. Since he entered his grandfather's name on his marriage certificate, it is possible that he never knew his real origin. His mother had left the country before her son turned 2 years old, thus making it easy for the grandparents, if they so desired, to suppress the information almost totally.

Hilary reports that when growing up the observant sisters were never conscious of any forbidden territory in their family history, nor did they sense the absence of any paternal relatives. Their mother's large family provided plenty of activities for them. Furthermore, she remembers asking no disquieting questions. Although she admits the possibility that her parents might have 'headed off' an embarrassing line of inquiry, none of her recollections confirms that hypothesis (Hilary Walton, personal interview, 9 May 1985).

Frederic's illegitimacy had several practical consequences. Hilary speculates that if he had known the truth about his birth, his sense of shame might well explain the somewhat nebulous role that he played in their family life (personal interview, 15 May 1986). All that one can know for certain, however, is that he must have had a lonely childhood, since the family that reared him was unusually small and unnaturally old. Perhaps in reaction, he chose for a wife a woman with nine siblings, and for many years lived harmoniously next door to his mother-in-law and her two unmarried daughters (VPE, 2). Since his wife had been born in Oswestry, their Shropshire home, her roots went deep. As a result, it was easy for her to take the lead in family life and to set the pace.

Frederic Pym is perhaps best described in constrast to his wife. Unlike her, he presented an outwardly respectable and conventional demeanour, whereas she was oblivious to fashion and absent-minded, like Jane Cleveland in *Jane and Prudence* (MS PYM 98, f. 117). Hilary describes her father as 'extremely good-tempered, undemanding and appreciative', virtues not commonly ascribed to fathers of that generation. His life, pleasant and not unduly demanding, centred around his profession as a gentlemanly solicitor, and in general Hilary describes an unruffled existence (VPE, 2–4).

In actual fact, then, Barbara's mother and her family of female relations were the influential figures in her early life. It is important to note that Barbara apparently took after her father more than she did her mother; according to her sister she was peace-loving by nature and quite unaggressive (personal interview, 15 May 1986). She must, furthermore, have been baffled by her mother's rejection of a traditionally feminine interest in clothing. Instead, Mrs Pym possessed a keen interest in golf, the source of Barbara's nickname for her, which was 'Links'. Mrs Pym's adventurous spirit is typified by the fact that she was once photographed riding a motorcycle (Hilary Walton, personal interview, 22 May 1986). Barbara, on the other hand, was always very interested in fashion and took great pride in her mastery of the domestic arts. Her diaries throughout her life contain constant references to sewing clothes and cooking meals. In one significant respect, however, Barbara differed from her father: she had far more literary interests and gifts than he. As he wrote her ruefully in 1950, he was surprised to find that he enjoyed *Some Tame Gazelle*, since his tastes ran more to thrillers (MS PYM 167, f. 56).

Along with the pleasures of Pym's early years, she learnt some negative lessons as well. Like many other creative people, she grew up feeling quite different from more ordinary people, but she decided very early on that everyday life, with its 'daily round' of housework, provided a necessary stability for her.[20] As a result, she turned her commitment to the quotidian into a protective shield, thereby resisting experimentation and change. Even more importantly, from childhood she developed a sense of her own unworthiness that accounts for her later disastrous romantic episodes. These misadventures were the result in part of her chronic tendency to overvalue love, a psychological phenomenon described by Karen Horney in *Feminine Psychology*.[21]

Life in a hierarchical society had taught Barbara that since men had pride of place, every woman needed a mate. She discerned, however, that without her busy mother and female friends, daily life in Oswestry would have been less comfortable. Yet for all their obvious competence, no woman seemed content to remain a spinster.[22] Husbands were deemed necessary to ensure an appropriate social position, and to protect oneself from the possible exploitation of vicars and curates, who—as depicted in Pym's early fictional fragments—seemed eager to beguile the poor spinster into a life of pointless servitude in exchange for a few words of praise (MS PYM 6, ff. 121, 160). The confusions inherent in this mixed message about social roles would have troubled any sensitive person, and Pym seemed to remain mired in contemplation of village life—and unable to leave home. She returned to Oswestry to live with her parents after going down from Oxford in 1934. Rather than leaving home and embarking on an independent life as her younger sister did, Barbara retreated to her childhood home and began the process of incorporating aspects of village life into her novels.[23] Her own ambivalence about this decision is shown in the fact that years later she was still offering explanations for these six years at home, as if aware that her behaviour needed some defence (MS PYM 98, f. 79).

Pym wrote about the qualities of village existence that had fascinated and troubled her as a child. For example, growing up next-door to two maiden aunts, one of whom was specially dear to her, made her well aware that being lovable was no guarantee of being marriageable. According to Hilary's recollection, as early as 1936, two years after going down from Oxford, Barbara began describing the antics of a Miss Moberley, a spinster character who eventually appeared in an unfinished spy novel (personal interviews, 9 May 1985, 15 May 1986; MS PYM 12, ff. 1–4).[24] It seems reasonable to assume that in 1936 the prospect of spinsterhood loomed large in Pym's life, since Henry Harvey, her Oxford lover, quite obviously had no intention of marrying her. Inventing an upper-class but comically outrageous older woman, who delights in interfering in everyone else's life, was an effective way of overcoming her own dread of being single. Imagining and magnifying the absurd details of such a life helped her to accept her own situation and to control the anxiety she might have felt about her own future. Thus she began a life-long habit of finding a comic literary receptacle for negative experiences, a process of conversion into which she channelled much of her creative energy. Later events suggest that the strategy was partly defensive in nature; more importantly, though, it did allow her to exercise her considerable talent as an artist. Consequently, in later years Pym, unlike the neurotic patients of Karen Horney, never permitted any emotional distress to interfere with the practice of her craft.

None the less, circumstances arose which severely tested Pym's self-control. Not only was Frederic Pym a less-than-positive model of masculinity in his daughters' childhood, but in later years his kindliness genuinely caused a family disaster. Although partial accounts of this incident appear in Barbara's journal, without Hilary's commentary it would have been difficult to interpret the scrappy entries. In 1945 'Links', Barbara's mother, died of cancer. Within a year Frederic had married a woman from a family of estate agents, about the time that Hilary's marriage had broken up. Barbara's only recorded reaction to the news reflects her valiant attempt to try to make the best of a series of shocks and changes, none of which was easy to accept. She wrote to Henry:

> I have so much news that I had better just fling it at you in Compton-Burnett style. Hilary and her husband have separated and my father has married again and given us a very nice step-mother of suitable age and a dear brother and sister, whom I have not met . . . It was all a great surprise I might add! Life seemed to be whirling too fast for us! (*VPE*, 180)

It is hard to believe that her father's remarriage could have pleased her much, since she still felt numb from the loss of her beloved mother. Her early manuscripts often included widows living contentedly with their spinster daughters, indicating that such a fantasy of the future had some meaning for her personally. After the marriage took place, however, she remained on pleasant terms with both her father and step-mother, although she rarely mentions them in her journals. Suddenly an enigmatic passage appears in her notebook on 3 November 1956 (I quote entire):

> Golfers in the dusk at Beaconsfield as I come back after this grim day. Dor's [her father] liabilities £12,000 or more. Assets—£600.
> That day, even if others come worse, won't ever be repeated again.
> A novel—to be written in the *very far* distant future—called the Grandparents—full of dreadful and surprising revelations—like that awful Dutch play.
> Monday I went to look up Link's will at Somerset House. She

left £9,954—all to Dor. Will dated 24 May 1912. (MS PYM 48, ff. 7–8)

According to Hilary's account, her solicitor father had lost most of his wife's money in unwise investments. Furthermore, he owed the bank £12,000 because he had been too generous in countersigning for some clients who needed second mortgages. When they defaulted, he owed the bank in their stead. The sisters felt it was incumbent upon them to pay off his debts and to make him a subsistence allowance (Hilary Walton, personal interviews, 9 May 1985, 15 May 1986). Since neither of them earned a great deal, the financial burden was considerable. (Barbara worked at the International African Institute in London, Hilary for the BBC).

Barbara's way of managing her feelings about this complicated situation was characteristic of her usual style, as subsequent diary entries indicate. Although the whole incident loomed large in her life for a time, by 8 November, five days later, she reports of better news 'and a lightening of the Cloud'. She then records a story she has heard about a woman who lost two rings at the Ladies Toilet (MS PYM 48, f. 8). Life appears to be back to normal and the bad news neutralized or contained. In spite of the resurgence of Barbara's saving sense of humour, the effect of her father's financial difficulties was a considerable long-term financial burden on the two underpaid sisters. Had Barbara been a more confident or rebellious woman in general, she might have found some means of expressing her justifiable anger. Instead, the whole affair contributed to vaguely unhappy feelings, hints of which appear in *A Glass of Blessings* and *No Fond Return of Love*.

In the context of Horney's psychological scheme, in childhood Pym's 'basic anxiety' caused her to develop an overly compliant personality; consequently, in her adult life she suffered from a kind of emotional paralysis that inhibited any desire to rebel.[25] Pym did indulge in a period of flamboyant adolescent behaviour, which occurred at the end of her school days and at Oxford (a period quite typical of the usual pattern for self-effacing people, according to Horney).[26] Her short period of ambition and experimentation, however, ended abruptly when she fell in love with Henry Harvey at Oxford

University. Thus the reason that Pym wrote perceptively about inhibited, conforming but acutely sensitive women was that she was one herself. At the same time, she possessed the rare capacity to generalize from and to transform her own feelings and experiences into more universal statements, while avoiding self-pity or whining. Further, she had the insight to understand that her own miseries were hardly unique. Others, therefore, might find solace or a sense of kinship from reading about such matters even though, as Letty in *Quartet in Autumn* states, 'the position of an unmarried, unattached, ageing woman is of no interest whatever to the writer of modern fiction' (*QA*, 3).

Although Pym was able to make artistic use of her plight, she could not resolve her personal dilemma. Her individual character was set in early childhood because, as Horney suggests, childhood is the time when we learn to conduct ourselves with appropriate flexibility, moving when necessary 'towards, against, or away from others'. Unfortunately, even as an adult Barbara exhibited some qualities of an anxious child, one who tends to respond in an excessive or rigid fashion so that 'Affection . . . becomes clinging; compliance becomes appeasement'.[27] Whenever she felt thwarted in love affairs, she found herself giving in far too easily to unreasonable demands. She was often too timid to fight for her basic rights, even though she was well aware that men she idealized did not respect her for her restraint. As a result, she often found herself unable to assert her own desires against her lovers' wishes. No amount of self-awareness could cure her of this habit. But the novels, particularly the early manuscripts, provided her a place in which she could defend and excuse herself for the failure she sensed in the way she was conducting her life. Writing provided an opportunity to regain a feeling of control. Indeed, the plot of 'Civil to Strangers', her second and still unpublished novel, can be read as a disguised method of obtaining revenge on Henry Harvey, the man who had nearly destroyed her self-esteem.[28]

In order to judge the impact of Barbara's loss of confidence after Oxford and her disappointment over Henry Harvey, it is helpful to contrast briefly her earliest efforts in fiction, written long before she had attempted to convert her fantasies of love into some semblance of reality. When she was about 9, her cousins and sister helped her perform her only opera, 'The Magic Diamond'. Although the problematical nature of marriage was to be a staple of her later fiction—'the war of genders' as Penelope Lively calls them—only in childhood did she write so candidly about her fears.[29]

Barbara based her plot on fairy-tale conventions and her lyrics rather loosely on Gilbert and Sullivan operas, which were familiar to her as a child because her parents had performed in several different operettas (VPE, 3). At the same time, even when allowing for the Gilbert and Sullivan influence, the peculiarities of Pym's opera are striking. The hero, Prince George, is told that since he has stolen the Wizard's magic, he must choose between having his head chopped off and seeking the Magic Diamond, a gem guarded by many dragons. Although the Prince's dilemma is not uncommon in fairy stories and myths, where the hapless hero usually trusts to blind luck and the help of friendly animals to rescue him from an otherwise sure death, in this situation Prince George is simply unable to choose.[30] Both fates seem so dire that he wants Rosebud (played, of course, by Barbara) to come tell him what to do. After a considerable amount of time, during which Rosebud sings 'How can I help him/for if he's killed/Who shall I marry/That is a difficult question', the Wizard tires of waiting. Fortuitously, he oversteps his bounds by claiming that the King had decreed that Rosebud should marry him, and the infuriated King has him taken off to prison (MS PYM 98, ff. 7–12).

The stalled action of the play violates all the conventions of fairy tales, which, as Bruno Bettelheim asserts, offer to the child models of successful behaviour. Usually the heroes venture into the world, find 'secure places' and meet their mates, the one person with whom one can live 'without ever again having to experience separation anxiety'.[31] Barbara clearly preferred the typical Gilbert and Sullivan plot, in which the happy ending is usually fortuitous rather than the result of heroic striving. Her choice, however, is significant; she emphasises that George and Rosebud cannot act because they are unable to choose. Apparently, her conviction that choices are inherently dangerous, no matter which one is selected, reflected some kind of inhibition in her ability even to imagine leaving home and becoming autonomous.

This humorous opera of childish inaction, with its resolution by parental fiat, contains the genesis of certain issues that were of life-long interest to its young author. Plots were never Pym's strong point, but the problem of finding and keeping a suitable mate (with its accompanying echoes of separation anxiety) surely was a recurring theme in her work. Because the young writer was blissfully unaware of the implications of her plot, she wrote quite candidly of her convictions: keeping secrets is an important but difficult task, and ultimately one solves problems not by powerful thoughts or actions but by powerful parents. Later on, when maturity increased her self-consciousness, she buried her convictions more expertly, but the issues of rivalry and power are deeply embedded in most of her plots.

By the time Pym turned 16, her work still contained fantasies of future life rather than mirroring her everyday existence. Her first completed novel manuscript, 'Young Men in Fancy Dress', shows the influence of the novels of Aldous Huxley, whose *Crome Yellow* offered an especially attractive model to her (MS PYM 96, f. 4). In following Huxley's lead, Pym was demonstrating his importance in the popular culture of the time as well as her own affinity for his style.

In his early novels Huxley writes airily about a society in which the usual rules of decorum have been suspended. Highborn characters indulge in sophisticated conversations about their illicit love affairs, while elderly eccentrics carry on their elaborate scientific experiments and debate seriously the possibility of proving or disproving the existence of God. Huxley's attitude is captured by his comically dispassionate tone. Nothing is treated entirely seriously. Politics are important only because fanatical leaders can exercise some mysterious sexual attractiveness (as in *Point Counter Point*); otherwise the rise of Fascism is subordinated to the importance of personal relations. To a young girl such as Pym, schooled never to discuss religion, politics or sex in polite society, Huxley's candour was irresistible.

From Huxley's example, Pym learnt that intelligence, especially the capacity for being articulate, was a form of power.

This explains why her hero in 'Young Men in Fancy Dress', the young poet Denis Feverel, is obsessed by the wonder of words. As an imitator, though, she was a little too young for her chosen plot. Often the tone seems breathless with anticipation for the adult life soon to be hers. Her imagination was dazzled by seemingly endless possibilities, and she created scenes of wild parties in a Chelsea she had never visited (MS PYM 98, f. 74). But for all her youth, she learnt from Huxley some fundamentals she never forgot. He taught her that what mattered in writing was establishing an individual voice, creating stimulating conversations and making the most of one's observations.

In view of Pym's early political opinions, such as the admiration she expressed for Germany and for Hitler's storm troopers in her diaries, letters and early manuscript versions of *Some Tame Gazelle* (MS PYM 2), one can only be grateful that she abandoned political themes early in her career. Her politics, however, were based on her private emotional needs, and did not reflect any commitment to the Nazi view of society.[32] In fact, her flirtations with Germans while she was in Europe on holiday offered a respite from the misery of being mistreated by Henry; it was no accident that she became enamoured of Germany and of German lovers at the time when Henry Harvey was treating her with disdain and contempt (MS PYM 102, ff. 55–8). Fortunately for the success of her career, she had the sense to realize that her literary strength had little to do with elaborate plots or philosophic discourses; therefore the frivolous atmosphere of Huxley's early novels particularly suited her style. In his novels and in her imitation, characters might suffer from unrequited love, but they never lost their taste for good meals, literary conversation, bad poetry and wonderfully irrelevant anecdotes. The detachment of Huxley's narrative style, the absence of a judgemental attitude and his genial humour became permanent features of Pym's own subsequent work.

Although Huxley's example helped Pym to gain confidence in her innate gifts, his model had some limitations for a young woman, especially one as vulnerable and sensitive as she. He expressed his hostile feelings towards women by placing them rigidly into categories. Even though many were based on the character of real people, they seem unrealistic. His character types include the *femme fatale* who ruthlessly uses her lovers (Lucy Tantamount in *Point Counter Point*), the hopeless and pitiful romantic (Mrs Aldwinkle in *Those Barren Leaves*), or the utterly engaging but not quite human female novelist, who when deserted by her lover 'safely laid [him] down in pickle, waiting to be consumed whenever she should be short of fictional provisions' (Mary Thriplow in the same novel).[33] Huxley's spirit of scientific detachment allowed him to make the most of his acute observations, but in the process of encapsulating his human specimens, any sensitivity to sexual passion disappears, an absence notable in Pym's novels as well. Real affection and tolerance in Huxley's fiction is aroused only by the behaviour of elderly males, eccentric relations who are totally absorbed by abstract intellectual speculations. For Huxley the loyalties of childhood were paramount, particularly the affection of brothers, a fact which accounts for the detachment with which his protagonists generally observe the disloyalty of lovers to each other.[34]

Pym, therefore, could not follow his example with complete success. For one thing, she was too young to be as detached from sexual passion as he was. Instead, she was torn between two desires: she knew her need to develop powers of observation for the sake of her writing career, but the aloofness that the role demanded was not compatible with her hopes of finding sexual love. Huxley's flippant references to illicit sex were part of a sophisticated veneer that appealed to the young girl. Unfortunately, living by his standards threatened her emotional equilibrium. To bridge the gap, she invented a new personality for herself, called Sandra. Although Hazel Holt describes Sandra as a uniquely dashing, daring and outgoing young woman, she was really a 1920s revival, an imitation of Huxley's *femme fatale*, Lucy Tantamount (*VPE*, 9). Given the disparity between Barbara's natural timidity and the pressures of that role, the resulting disasters were sadly predictable.

For most people, inventing or assuming a new identity is either uncommon or a sign of mental deterioration, but in Barbara's case inventing roles, for herself or her family, was quite routine. Since as a child she had named her parents Links and Dor, renaming herself at a moment when her life offered her unknown and perhaps frightening challenges was a natural response (*VPE*, 3). Hazel Holt's description of Pym's joyful reaction to Oxford effectively captures the pleasures of freedom the university life offered her; but freedom can bring with it great anxiety, especially if one's fantasies and conversation outstrip one's real desires (*VPE*, 9). To compensate for feeling inadequate, the often painfully shy Barbara deliberately forced herself to act like her exact opposite. Sandra's wildness and volatility kept Barbara very busy, thereby obscuring her internal conflicts and artificially quieting her anxieties. Her strategy, moreover, kept her from becoming aware of her real feelings, while her extraverted behaviour encouraged the advances of young men, who expected her to be able to live up to her reputation.

Most other young women of Barbara's generation successfully avoided sexual entanglement at an early age. The pressures of social convention, university regulations and parental disapproval discouraged early sexual experimentation. But Barbara had two distinct disadvantages: not only did she lack confidence in her own charms, but she admired masculine aggression. As a result, she rejected the men who expressed tender feelings for her, and pursued abjectly those who did not love her (Hilary Walton, personal interview, 9 May 1985). Had she not felt overwhelmed by her unexpected physical attraction to Henry Harvey, furthermore, she might have negotiated the pitfalls of romantic intrigue with more success.

Instead, she risked making a fool of herself. As it turned out, her friends did not discard her in spite of her obsessive interest in romantic attachments. In fact, her excesses provided a source of excitement and a focus for their lives. She contrived to involve those closest to her in all her imaginative games throughout her life. As a child, her fantasies entertained her family (Hilary Walton, personal interview, 9 May 1985). At Oxford her friends helped her track down the men she selected, and in middle age her friends did the same (*VPE*, xiv).

Pym's eccentricities made her noticeable but not objectionable, because university students, whose own sense of identity is by no means secure, often find such behaviour appealing.

She acted out the confusion they internalized. The powerful appeal to her friends of her fantasies can be demonstrated by the fact that Mary Sharp, a St Hilda's contemporary, reported dreaming of Robert Liddell's death, a fact which suggests an extraordinary degree of identification with Barbara's life (MS PYM 102, f. 22). Pym's friends became absorbed in her romantic world; they willingly abetted her efforts to track her man of the hour by reporting their sightings of her chosen prey. Her early diaries contain her record of observations and abound with references to the attractive men she saw. Whenever she spotted a likely candidate, she would attempt to discover his name by following him to his lodgings, and if necessary she looked him up in the Oxford calendar, which listed the undergraduates. Quite clearly she did not expect the man to pursue her.

On the intellectual side, Oxford disappointed Pym, although she never admitted it. To some extent her frivolity, so well captured by Janice Rossen in her essay 'Love in the Great Libraries', was an understandable reaction to the rigidity of the Oxford English schools.[35] The curriculum was divided between literature, in which she read widely, and linguistics, which she disliked. Because she lacked interest in Old Norse Sagas, *Beowulf* or Old English, she could not really compete for a first-class degree.

Her reaction to her predicament was, unfortunately, all too characteristic. Instead of complaining or even thinking about the problem, she sought to distract herself by the pleasant pastime of man-chasing.[36] In some ways her strategy worked. She avoided fruitless resentment and rebelliousness while gaining some literary experience by dramatizing her adventures in her diaries. At the same time, she knew that she could have done much better scholastically, and as late as 1976, she felt that she should have pursued an academic career with more seriousness (*VPE*, 287).[37]

The diaries, however, were much more than mere distraction, because they also served an important role in her development as a writer. They represent Pym's experiment with romantic, egocentric fiction, but by this time she was no longer the open child who had invented Princess Rosebud many years before. Experiencing the pangs of unrequited love, further-more, is more devastating than writing theoretically about such misery as she had done in 'Young Men in Fancy Dress'. Falling in love with Henry Harvey, whom she called at various times both Gabriel and Lorenzo in her diaries, had made her painfully aware of her limitations. To her distress, she found herself in the uncomfortable role of the victim, but this time no powerful parents could rescue her.

Pym's natural talent, however, was for comedy, not ro-mance. Fortunately for the success of her career, she purged herself—at least in fiction—of her self-pity by indulging it thoroughly in her diaries. The two times during which she kept extensive personal records were from 1932 to 1938 and from 1943 to 1945 following the failure of her romances with Henry Harvey and Gordon Glover, moments of extreme misery for her (MSS PYM 101–3, 108–10). Among other things, the diaries allowed her to ventilate her depressed feelings and slowly to regain her sense of humour and detach-ment as she began to enjoy the process of word-making they entailed.

In the Oxford diaries we can see the continuation of Pym's literary apprenticeship. Like those of Denton Welch, whose journals Pym later read with admiring obsessiveness, they are a chronicle, according to the classifications of Thomas Mallon.[38] Even if all diaries are, as Mallon attests, written for an audience, her forthright habit of addressing the reader as the 'Gentle Reader in the Bodleian' is unusual (VPE, 104). Like many chroniclers she is not introspective, nor does she question her behaviour or her motives. Instead she describes a series of dramatic scenes without much comment, indicating that she never learnt a great deal from the disasters that befell her.[39] Pym may express mortification at her ineptness at times, but her feelings reflect more shame and humiliation than guilt and self-doubt.[40] When she recounts events, she self-consciously makes a good story to entertain herself and her audience.

The Saga of Lorenzo, the pursuit that absorbed her during her university days, is really an unsuccessful romantic quest, in which Pym, no longer under parental protection like Princess Rosebud, suffers from the pangs of love typical of both courtly love tradition and of the biblical account of Jacob's long servitude for his beloved Rachel. Since Pym is very aware of her literary sources and analogues, she comments quite proudly upon her seven years of service to Henry (*VPE*, 58). Fortunately for her, her love of literature was deeply genuine, and provided her with an important alternative to the romance she sought so eagerly. She simply could not resist turning her adventures into a series of dramatic scenes in which she starred.

Just how much of Pym's romantic adventures were fantasy, and how many really happened is, of course, impossible to know.[41] Two factors cast doubt on the veracity of her accounts: the first is the reaction of two of her close friends, Honor Wyatt and Robert Liddell, and the second is the vague and inexact way in which Pym describes her sexual encounters. In the first instance, her friends—both of whom tend to patronize her to different degrees because she treated them as mother-figures—say that she tended to exaggerate the significance of her relationships. Even the admiring Rupert Gleadow, her first serious Oxford lover, wrote to her that he never took her feelings about Henry Harvey very seriously in spite of what she had told him about that affair (MS PYM 150, f. 97). Honor Wyatt felt that Barbara had dramatized the importance of her much later affair with Honor's estranged husband Gordon Glover (interview, BBC, 3 July 1987). Finally, Robert Liddell, in whom Pym confided her misery over Henry Harvey, disputes the idea that her relationship with Harvey could properly be called an 'affair'.[42] Probably the vague and unsatisfactory way in which Pym describes her adventures results both from an extreme inhibition and a tendency to exaggerate and romanticize unsatisfactory events. Fundamental to her character was a need for privacy; she believed in keeping her problems to herself and in presenting a pleasant demeanour to the world. In numerous diary entries, she comments proudly that she had hidden her anger from the person who had aroused it most intensely.

Her cheerful appearance was not an obvious deception but a necessity to her sense of self. Unfortunately, friends misinterpreted the meaning of her serenity; Hazel Holt said that the apparently effortless good humour of her friend and colleague

Barbara made it almost impossible to believe that she had ever repressed anger or felt depressed. Instead she remembered Barbara's frivolity and cheerfulness as transcending her self-control (personal interview, 22 May 1985). Pym's affability, however, was somewhat deceptive: because she made a concerted effort whenever possible to distance herself from pain, she appeared to be unmarked by unpleasant experiences. Under the circumstances it was not surprising that her friends made the mistake of underestimating the cost of her struggles.

Her long-range methods of handling suffering are best illustrated by examining her relationship with Rupert Gleadow. Although as Hazel Holt insists, Barbara's long but fruitless relationship with Henry Harvey permanently changed the direction of her life and undermined her confidence, her earlier misadventures with Rupert offer a glimpse into her sexual difficulties and into her life-long method of converting her emotional disasters into novels (Hazel Holt, personal interview, 22 May 1985).

Rupert was unusual in the pantheon of Pym's lovers because he was always more physically attracted to her than she was to him. Before he took an interest in her, men in her life had either been distant fantasy figures or friends whose interest she spurned (MS PYM 101). In the beginning stages of their romance, however, Pym seemed happy in Rupert's company. Unfortunately, the pleasures of being in love with love made her miss the warning signals that appeared: not only did the intensity of their feelings differ, but the slight disparity in their ages meant that they were in different stages of their lives. Barbara at 19 was still flighty; whereas Rupert, being older, was eager to prove his manhood, a proposition most young women of that era found quite resistible.[43] As Rossen notes, Pym's character had a strong split between a romantic side, exemplified by her Sandra persona, and a more analytical one.[44] This division further ensured that she could not be enticed into being his mistress merely to make Rupert feel like a man. The disparity of their desires, therefore, is obvious from the start. Fairly early on in their relationship she reported, 'He was very Theocritean and loving. I got a wee bit sick of it—but tried to please him as I was determined to treat him as kindly as possible as he'd Schools on the 9th' (VPE, 14). Complying with his wishes so that he would do well in examinations suggests an absence of physical passion on her part, but she ignored such thoughts.

Throughout the happy days of enjoying Rupert's attentions, though, Barbara continued to record her thoughts about other men, moments of equal importance to her (MS PYM 101, f. 31–7). During the long vacation Rupert's visit to her home had fateful consequences. Responding to the intensity of their time spent together—at one point Barbara records watching him take a bath—Rupert suggested that they go to bed together (MS PYM 101, f. 42). Although she was gratified by the suggestion, she refused:

> we had much fun and a fight over that. It was a very cold evening . . . but we went down Weston Lane and looked at the stars. I said that the happiness one got out of love was worth any unhappiness it might (and generally does) bring. I can't remember what Rupert said but he wasn't so sure about it not having had the experience I suppose. (*VPE*, 16–17)

Considering her relatively limited experience of life at this point, her pessimism about the pains of love may seem premature, but later events proved her prescient.

On returning to Oxford, Rupert pressed his suit with dire consequences. Whatever Pym wrote then no longer exists, since she subsequently removed those pages from her diary, leaving only a poignant fragment of the original: 'Today I must always remember I suppose. I went to tea with Rupert (and ate a pretty colossal one)—and he with all his charm, eloquence and masculine viles, persuaded . . .' (*VPE*, 17). The complete absence of detail of subsequent meetings suggests that Barbara was blotting out a painful memory. Twelve days after the event, the dutiful chronicler records, 'spent afternoon Rupert but can't remember what I did. Shall have to consult him about this' (MS PYM 101, f. 46). Such amnesia testifies both to her lack of serious interest in him and to her unhappiness about the way things turned out.

Pym was evasive about the event, and her entries leave the impression that their friendship trailed off gradually. But Rupert's method of confronting misery was different. Two days after the disaster, he wrote to her explaining that his delay in corresponding was purposeful. He hoped to give her a chance to ponder their extraordinary behaviour: the complete absence of any sexual passion in bed. He expressed regret that he had found it necessary to threaten her in order to ensure her co-operation and acknowledged that she would no doubt refuse to repeat the experiment. His chief sadness was that he feared that she had not enjoyed any part of the process. He expressed a desire to have her in his bed merely for the pleasure of her company and in general seemed very affectionate. At the letter's end, he closed with the hope that the archangel Gabriel would guard her since he could not be there himself (MS PYM 150, f. 13–16).

The contrast between Rupert's letters and Barbara's vague diary entries suggest that although his attachment was the stronger, he was the more capable of facing defeat than she, largely because he could attribute the failure to Barbara's unwillingness. Even after the failed seduction, he made further references to her commitment to her virginity and mocked her worries about possible pregnancy, unnecessary he thought, since he was prepared to use birth control. Even though he declared that he would gladly accept her virginity as a birthday present, by that time he had obviously lost hope that such an event would occur (MS PYM 150, f. 59). Gradually his letter writing tapered off, their meetings diminished in number, and by the next term Barbara had a new love interest, Henry Harvey, whose unkind treatment of her caused her endless anguish for the next few years.

Two subsequent matters suggest the importance of the event. First, Barbara told Hilary that she had had an affair with Rupert, which under the circumstances seems to have been an exaggeration (personal interview, 9 May 1985). Second, in 1940, when the thought of Rupert no longer caused her pain, she incorporated aspects of her own disaster into her description of a comically portrayed fiasco, the elopement of Francis Cleveland and Barbara Bird in *Crampton Hodnet*. In the novel, Barbara Bird literally runs out of the hotel room they plan to share in Dover.

The whole question of Pym's sexual adventures is important precisely because of the insight that they can give us into her attempts to manage her feelings. By observing her response, we can better understand the forces that made her a writer, yet which at the same time inhibited her full development as an artist and as a woman.

Pym was well aware of her own methods, procedures she described in a fragment called 'Beatrice Wyatt or the Lumber Room'. The heroine, Beatrice Wyatt, says that the memory of a past love is like a storage room or attic, 'a kind of lumber room—full of old pictures'. After a long period of tip-toeing past the room, it is safe to open the door and inspect the shrouded object. The passage of time has converted the painful love into 'mild kindly looks and spectacles. Nothing to be afraid of anymore'. The explanation she gives for the change is that 'the lumber room like death was a great leveller' (MS PYM 6, f. 149).

Understanding the metaphor of the lumber room makes it possible for us to observe Pym's creative process. Unpleasant experiences with men, such as the failure with Rupert, were not matters to be examined carefully and introspectively. Instead of dissecting the events, or pondering why her flirtatious manner could not obliterate her basic shyness, she turned her attention in another direction, that of pursuing other men. At the same time, the lumber room was a harmful and deathlike experience. In the process of denying her feelings, some of them were destroyed altogether. Only after the passage of several years was it possible for her to write with detached humour about the inhibitions of a young Oxford scholar, who like Pym herself, ran away from a sexual encounter and embroidered her heroic account for the benefit of a woman friend.[45]

Perhaps in reaction to the aura of sexual deprivation and unexpressed misery that emanates from *Crampton Hodnet*, Anita Brookner in her review of the novel complained that Pym ruthlessly suppressed the sexual energies of her character Barbara Bird. Brookner had no way of knowing that Pym was drawing on her own experience, not deliberately inhibiting her character. What the cluster of events represents is a pattern that was repeated often in Pym's life: she experienced a painful emotional failure, the meaning of which she refused to contemplate. Later she chose to describe the event in more positive terms to her sister. After the passage of time, she was able to incorporate the whole matter into a comic episode in which she recounted the events with a surprising amount of honesty, irony and detachment.[46] In turn, the pervading sense of emotional deprivation which marks the story aroused the ire of a reviewer, who objected to the amount of denial, defensiveness and unhappiness that the entire literary strategy involved.

Pym was only partly aware of her part of the pattern, and was unwilling or unable to break from its constraints. Its convoluted history accounts for the remarkable quality of her ironic humour, her championing of spinsters and outsiders, and her ability to survive in spite of deprivation and disappointment, but it also marks the limits of her growth as a human being and as a novelist.

Notes

1. Nicholas Spice, 'Costa del Pym', review of *Crampton Hodnet, London Review of Books*, 4 July 1985, p. 10.
2. Anita Brookner, 'The Loneliness of Miss Pym', review of *Crampton Hodnet*, in *Sunday Times* (London), 23 June 1985, p. 11.
3. See Janice Rossen, 'Love in the Great Libraries: Oxford in the Work of Barbara Pym', *Journal of Modern Literature*, July 1985, pp. 285–6. She believes that Belinda abases herself to Henry so that Pym can apologize for her demonstrative nature. However, even in the early version Belinda makes fun of him. In *No Fond Return of Love* Dulcie's pursuit of Aylwin Forbes to a Somerset hotel imitates and betters Pym's experience. Pym tracked her neighbours for several years, following one of them to a similar hotel (MS PYM 91, f. 6–7). *The Sweet Dove Died*, written just after Richard Roberts, or Skipper, had rejected her, includes much material in early drafts, the Rose novel, from Pym's own life (MS PYM 26–8). Also, Leonora's final rejection of James reverses Skipper's desertion of her (*VPE*, 240–3).
4. Distaste for Pym's *oeuvre* appears, for instance, in Paul Ableman's review of *The Sweet Dove Died*, 'Genteelism', *Spectator*, 8 July 1978, p. 26, and in Marilyn Butler's 'Keeping up with Jane Austen', review of *An Unsuitable Attachment*, in *London Review of Books*, 6–19 May 1982, pp. 16–17. Favourable reviews include A.N. Wilson, 'St Barbara-in-the-Precinct', rev. *An Unsuitable Attachment*, *Spectator*, 20 February 1982, pp. 22–3 and Philip Larkin, 'The World of Barbara Pym', *Times Literary Supplement*, 11 March 1977, p. 260.
5. Rossen points out that Pym's heroines do likewise: they turn the dull

men they know into heroic figures ('Love in the Great Libraries', p. 279).

6. Wilson, p. 22.
7. Unlike most eccentrics, Pym was not a loner. Her friends and relatives joined in her obsessions because they found them amusing.
8. At present Mrs Holt is working on a biography of Pym.
9. See especially Frederick M. Keener, 'Barbara Pym Herself and Jane Austen', *Twentieth Century Literature* 31 (spring 1985): 89–110.
10. Butler, pp. 16–17.
11. Michael S. Howard, *Jonathan Cape Publisher* (London: Jonathan Cape, 1971), pp. 270–3.
12. Howard, pp. 285–7. Her publishers were motivated by business interests. They had no idea of her potential readership and ignored the increase in the number of single people, a significant group of potential admirers of her work. Tom Maschler, the new Cape director, admitted in 1977 that he had never read one of her books (MS PYM 169, f. 194).
13. Some publishers recognized her talent, but *Some Tame Gazelle* was not accepted until 1949 (MS PYM 163, ff. 43–7). Only one of her stories was published before her rediscovery (MS PYM 163, f. 1–42).
14. Marvellously strange letters come from fans: one from a woman saying she had been born upside down and had been like that ever since (MS PYM 169, f. 191–3).
15. [*Editor's note:* This note of dull depression can also be detected in the fact that Dulcie is not particularly satirized by the narrator for her adolescent infatuations. It seems perfectly reasonable within the context of the novel that she should haunt Aylwin Forbes as part of her 'research' (*NFR*, 44). Pym seems unable to find this aspect of her heroine amusing, even mildly shocking.]
16. *The Sweet Dove Died* represented a significant change in Pym's style, but publishers feared it would not sell well enough (MS PYM 165, ff. 6, 10). Larkin suggested that Pym try to get her old copyrights back so as to entice a new publisher, who could make money from the reprints (MS PYM 151, ff. 60–1). In 1976 and 1977, publishers had once again rejected another of Pym's novels, *Quartet in Autumn* (*VPE*, 288, 293).
17. Robert J. Graham, 'Cumbered with Much Serving: Barbara Pym's "Excellent Women"', *Mosaic* 17 (1984), p. 154.
18. Walter Clemons, 'An Unnoticed World', review of *A Glass of Blessings*, in *Newsweek* (14 April 1980), p. 96.
19. In 1943, Pym sentimentalized over an old wedding photograph of Gordon and Honor, calling them 'the two people I love best in the world' (*VPE* 140).
20. Pym wrote a curious short story, 'The Vicar Floating By', probably in 1941 (MS PYM 99, ff. 24–44). In this tale, the two Pomfret sisters become Surrealists and move to London, where Agatha becomes obsessed by her art. Only the vicar's arrival can restore her to sanity. He brings them both back to the village. The story indicates that Pym purposefully avoided using her 'subconscious' in her art.

21. Karen Horney, *Feminine Psychology* (1967; rpt New York: W.W. Norton, 1973), p. 185.
22. Although Pym was impressed by the energy and powerfulness of women in her childhood, in adulthood she sometimes objected to life with 'Too Many Women' (Janice Rossen, *The World of Barbara Pym*, London: Macmillan, 1987, Ch. 3).
23. Hilary defended Barbara's choice, noting that it was both a common and a practical decision. She saved money by living at home (personal interview, 15 May 1986). At the same time, the results were regressive, much as a similar behaviour on the part of Helena Napier in *Excellent Women* represents a 'symbolic regression' (Rossen, *The World of Barbara Pym*, p. 120). Living at home kept Pym from establishing an independent adult life. Instead, she clung to old friends and old haunts. When the war forced her to leave, she gained extra weight while she agonized about what to do (MS PYM 107, f. 79). She survived the uprooting by immediately attaching herself to Honor Wyatt and her family.
24. Miss Moberly was the name of the former principal of St Hilda's, who had retired shortly before Pym went up (*St Hilda's College Register: 1893–1972* (Oxford: Bocardo & Church Army Press, 1977), p. 1).
25. Karen Horney, *Neurosis and Human Growth: The Struggle Toward Self-Realization* (1950; New York: W.W. Norton, 1970), pp. 18–19.
26. Horney, *Neurosis*, p. 222.
27. *Ibid.*, pp. 18–19.
28. Belinda in *Some Tame Gazelle* and Cassandra in 'Civil to Strangers' comment upon and excuse their own self-effacing behaviour (MS PYM 2, f. 235; MS PYM 5, ff. 154–5). As Pym aged, her patience wore thinner. Although she prided herself on hiding her fury from Richard Roberts, eventually she realized that he feared her (*VPE*, 235, MS PYM 160, f. 170).
29. Penelope Lively, 'Recent Fiction', *Encounter* 58 (April 1982), p. 76.
30. See Bruno Bettelheim, who comments that fairy tales 'guide the child ... to relinquish his infantile dependency wishes and achieve a more satisfying independent existence'. (*The Uses of Enchantment: The Meaning and Importance of Fairy Tales* (New York: Alfred Knopf, 1976), p. 11).
31. Bettelheim, p. 11.
32. Robert Liddell, 'Two Friends: Barbara Pym and Ivy Compton-Burnett', review of *A Very Private Eye*, in *London Magazine* (Aug./Sept. 1984), p. 63.
33. Aldous Huxley, *Those Barren Leaves* (London: Chatto & Windus, 1925), p. 359.
34. Philip West, 'Brothers under the Skin: Aldous and Julian Huxley', *Blood Brothers: Siblings as Writers*, ed. Norman Kiell (New York: International Universities Press, 1983), p. 167.
35. Janice Rossen, 'Love in the Great Libraries'.
36. Pym's reaction to her plight turned out to be characteristic of her later behaviour as well (see note 1 above). Her intrusive activities quieted the

discomfort caused by being trapped by forces beyond her control, and ultimately provided some material for her books, such as the homosexual couple Piers and Keith in *A Glass of Blessings* and Dulcie's tracking of Aylwin Forbes in *No Fond Return of Love*.

37. Ultimately, success allowed her to answer that question. Reviewer Nicholas Shrimpton reads *A Few Green Leaves* as an apologia for Pym's professional choice because the heroine, Emma Howick, discards her academic role to become a novelist. Nicholas Shrimpton, 'Bucolic Bones', review of *A Few Green Leaves*, in *New Statesman* (15 Aug. 1980), p. 17.

38. Thomas Mallon, *A Book of One's Own: People and Their Diaries* (1984; New York: Penguin, 1986), pp. xvi–xvii.

39. Mallon comments that writers like Pym find it easier 'to observe the life around [them] than to confide the one inside [them] to the diaries' (p. 37).

40. Pym copied out a quotation from Logan Pearsall Smith's *Trivia* in her Commonplace book, a passage which aptly describes a self-conscious person who becomes mortified by the memory of his extraverted behaviour (MS PYM 83, f. 36).

41. Although Pym knew which entries were factual, the reader can easily become confused.

42. Liddell, 'Two Friends', p. 59. In view of the exaggerated version of Pym and Harvey that appears in Liddell's novel *An Object for a Walk* (1966), one hesitates to accept completely his interpretation of events.

43. Rupert wanted an affair but complained in a letter that Oxford was an impossible place to have a mistress. Later he reported that other girls he knew shared Pym's suburban attitudes towards sex. He sensed that Pym feared she would be seduced the following term regardless of her desires (MS PYM 150, ff. 59–60, 83).

44. Rossen, 'Love in the Great Libraries', p. 283.

45. Because she delights in Sarah's flattering attention, Barbara Bird does not correct her mistaken impression that Barbara's relationship with Francis was sexual. Pym clearly understands the feelings that stimulate Barbara to further misrepresentations (MS PYM 10, ff. 263–5). The passage was cut from the published novel because, although of biographical interest, it did not work well dramatically.

46. Rossen points out that Catherine Oliphant in *Less than Angels* does not begin to mature as a writer until she can convert her personal misery about Tom's rejection of her into material for a story (Rossen, *The World of Barbara Pym*, Ch. 6). Pym based this point on herself.

Chapter 3

The Home Front: Barbara Pym in Oswestry, 1939–1941

HAZEL HOLT

From late 1939 until December 1941 Barbara Pym was living with her parents in Oswestry. It was not unusual in those days for a girl in her mid-twenties still to be at home, without any sort of job. But Barbara was not simply the Edwardian unmarried daughter at home (though there would have been some in her circle of acquaintances)—she was a writer. The fact that she was fortunate enough to have parents who were sufficiently well-off to feed and house her and give her a small allowance (well under £100 a year, which she supplemented by selling some of her books and old clothes) did not make her feel any less a professional author. That, she felt convinced, was to be her career: 'After supper I did some more writing which quells my restlessness—that is how I must succeed.'[1]

The trivial round of a small provincial town—the few mild domestic tasks, a little home dressmaking, church-going, an occasional bridge party or dance, was not really enough to absorb her interest and stretch her mind, even when supplemented by voracious reading and enthusiastic cinema-going.

> Went to Liverpool. Bought dull turkis [turquoise] wool material, black lace for evening blouse, white lace blouse, 6 silver buttons, white and gold evening bag.[2]

> In the evening went to see Bette Davis [sic] in *Dark Victory*, a very unhappy film but no tears from me.[3]

Read *Letters to Byron*. I am just the age Caro Lamb was when she first met him.[4]

Cleared out the bathroom cupboard as usual on Bank Holiday. In the evening Hugh Sinclair in *The Four Just Men*.[5]

Shopping in Shrewsbury. Lunch at Boots. Bought a puce jumper.[6]

In all day knitting and finishing *Mansfield Park*.[7]

There was material there for her novels—human nature may be observed as well in a microcosm as in the wider world—and Barbara had already recorded much of it in her first draft of *Some Tame Gazelle*; but she badly needed some new impetus. In 1938 she had gone, briefly, to Poland to work as a governess, but because of the political crisis she had had to return almost immediately. When she returned, she had hoped to live in London, sharing a flat with her sister Hilary, who was just about to start work at the BBC. But in September 1939 the war came and Barbara felt she had to go back to be with her parents in Oswestry. Life would never be quite the same again for anyone.

The effects were marginal at first—improvising blackout and preparing for evacuees, a few shortages and economies. It was still the time of the Phoney War.

Another long, busy day, moving beds, blacking out windows, etc. Into my mind came irrelevant past happinesses. About six o'clock the five evacuee children arrived.[8]

I had a dull day at home mostly telling the children not to do things. Still I shall be lucky if the worst this war can make me feel is boredom.[9]

Had our National Registration cards. Budget out—cigarettes up—Players 1s 1d to 1s 2d—and income tax. All drawing in our horns. Tried on some evening frocks and wondered when I should ever be able to wear them again. Depressed about the economies and the frightfulness and hopelessness of this or any war.[10]

Put in bulbs—hyacinths. Reading a biography of Caroline of Brunswick. Listened to *Bandwagon* [a radio programme]. This is a war diary, but this is, or seems to be, our life![11]

There was still cinema-going:

'Went to the pictures for the first time since war started. Took gasmasks but felt rather silly! Constance Bennett and Alice Faye in *Tail Spin*.'[12] And news of her friends: 'A postcard from Don [Liddell] to say that Jock and the Harveys are leaving Finland! Flight from the Bolsheviks in an open boat. Somehow, though it's serious, I can't help laughing.'[13]

Gradually the tempo quickened and by July 1940, after Dunkirk and with a very real threat of invasion, the war seemed very close indeed.

Grave news from France. The Germans have got Arras and Amiens. Day of National Prayer. Church packed morning and evening. Two fine services. I thought—Friedbert [a former German boy friend], against this, you haven't a chance.[14]

Desperate fighting on the Western Front. Dor [her father] went to L.D.V. [Home Guard] meeting.[15]

France is in desperate straits. We must prepare for the worst.[16]

Today at 1 p.m. we heard that France had given up. But honestly the news didn't make me feel afraid.[17]

I have joined the A.R.P. The countryside is lovely. Honeysuckle in the hedges. How *dare* the Nazis think they could invade it![18]

There was a great proliferation of voluntary services and English gentlewomen of all ages responded enthusiastically. Now perfectly ordinary people were doing the most extraordinary things, and never noticing just how extraordinary they were:

I was sitting by the fire writing when the siren went about 6:20. I got my things and rushed to the hospital where a great crowd of A.R.P. workers turned up and we had quite a jolly night with cups of tea and some sleep on the floor. The All Clear went about 4:30 a.m. The next night the sirens went at 8 and the All Clear at 5 a.m. It seemed as if we had never left this place—the Surrealists have nothing on us for odd situations![19]

Had just got undressed (11:30) when the sirens went. A cold night

with lovely clusters of searchlights. We were at the First Aid Post
until 4 a.m. Merseyside and Belfast got it.[20]

Waited up for the siren and it went at midnight. Fewer people at
the Post so it was cooler. Lying on the floor reading *The Scholar
Gipsy*. Home 4:45 a.m. Dawn and the first bird song.[21]

In the evening an anti-gas lecture—terrifying, but it's better to
know about it. Went into the tear-gas van—the snouted figures.
Got my badge.[22]

There were times when Excellent Women needed physical
as well as moral courage: 'Had a lovely letter from Rosemary
telling me how she was buried in the ruins of her flat. Now one
has heroes and heroines for friends who before were just
ordinary people!'[23]

As well as her A.R.P. work at the First Aid Post, Barbara
helped with the babies at the Clinic:

Busy at the Clinic weighing babies and learned the workings of a
baby's gas helmet. Was shown a (suspected) grown-together
fracture in a baby's leg and a swollen ankle. I am gradually
learning to pick up a baby with a nonchalant air.[24]

More congenial was her work at the YMCA camp for
soldiers, Parkhall, where she worked in the canteen. As well as
helping with the cash ('Did my nails with Pink Clover but later,
doing the money, it all peeled off'[25]) she also served at the
counter.

The cakes came late and there was a great scrum.[26]

Busy poaching eggs in neat little machines and later at the
counter.[27]

There were plenty of 'Pym' situations: 'General atmosphere
of *Umbrage* among Y.M. staff.'[28]

Susceptible as ever, Barbara found many attractive new
faces among the soldiers at the camp:

Went to Parkhall. There is a beautiful Pre-Raphaelite L/Bdr

[Lance Bombadier]! I was smiling to myself all morning as I thought of this.[29]

At the camp Desmond, all violet-brilliantine, rode my bicycle round the field. He took my magenta chiffon scarf and put his identity disc in its place. And now I wear it. Very busy evening and they were all singing 'When I grow too old to dream'.[30]

And, more seriously, there was a young Scot called Stewart, for whom she tried to learn Gaelic:

I was able to get back for a walk with Stewart. We had tea at the Coach and Dogs then went to the pictures, and afterwards learned more Gaelic. *Mo run feal, dileas*.[31]

Went out to tea with Stewart. We had from 5–6:30 together. I think I really will miss him.[32]

A beautiful sunny day but melancholy at Parkhall with so many gone. The Flowers of the Forest are a 'wede awa'.[33]

With her usual preoccupation with food, Barbara records several meals (poached eggs, spaghetti and mince pies; curried eggs; eggs, beans and cheese) as well as the occasional piece of good fortune: 'Links [her mother] managed to get a 7 lb jar of marmalade—such are the joys of going without. Not even love is so passionately longed for.'[34]

In addition to her frequent cinema-going, Barbara read continuously, and her taste was refreshingly catholic: Jane Austen's *Northanger Abbey*, Aldous Huxley's *After Many a Summer*, Pamela Hansford Johnson's *Girdle of Venus*, Thackeray's *Vanity Fair*, R.C. Hutchinson's *The Fire and the Wood*, John Piper's *Oxfordshire Guide*, Charlotte Brontë's *Villette*, Rosamond Lehmann's *Invitation to the Waltz*, Rex Warner's *The Aerodrome*, Angela Thirkell's *Before Lunch*, Tolstoy's *Anna Karenina*, E.M. Forster's *Howards End*, Llewelyn Powys's *Love and Death*, Virginia Woolf's *To the Lighthouse*, E.F. Benson's *As We Were* and ('something to look forward to') Ivy Compton-Burnett's *Parents and Children*.

Just occasionally she felt dissatisfied and uncertain:

Busy in the house and wondering (as I sometimes do) whether I ought not to be doing other things—leading a fuller life as one might say. But that passes.[35]

Poopa [Hilary] arrived about 7:30 in her car. She does have fun. I was frankly envious of her life this evening. She had some black Russian cigarettes![36]

Gave myself some beauty treatment. Feeling quite contented, especially when I can write a little.[37]

For several years, then, Barbara was gradually bringing into focus her own unique view of life. Like Angela Thirkell in her wartime novels and E.M. Delafield in *The Provincial Lady in Wartime*, she recorded the new and often absurd situations around her. As an Oxford graduate (something of a *rara avis* in Oswestry) she was, to some extent, outside the social circle in which her family moved. Hilary was away in Bristol by then, and although deeply involved in the activity around her, Barbara was able to view it with the dispassionate eye of a novelist. From 1938 until 1941 Barbara kept only small pocket diaries, such as are ordinarily used to record appointments. Barbara's entries were almost as brief, but as has been shown by these extracts, they were often pungent and original, encapsulating in a half-sentence a mood or an incident:

At the camp. Mr le Toussel cannot remember the colour of his wife's eyes and thinks that one is really civilised when one can see *Vogue*.[38]

Day of prayer. I went to church at 8 and (rather unsuitably) discovered a new 20 packet of Players [cigarettes] in my fur coat pocket during the service.[39]

Reading *To the Lighthouse*. Curious and beautiful. Very wet and dark afternoon. But oh what other Fridays there have been! Busy cleaning out the little pantry. *Sic transit . . .*[40]

She was also writing fiction, no matter how tired she was or how busy. She finished and revised her North Oxford novel, *Crampton Hodnet*:

Worked hard at my North Oxford novel and at knitting a balaclava.[41]

Determined to finish my North Oxford novel and sent it on the rounds.[42]

Making a second version of my North Oxford novel to send to Jock [Robert Liddell].[43]

Barbara also revised *Some Tame Gazelle*:

Sat in the garden reading *Some Tame Gazelle* which now seems crude and too full of obscure literary allusions.[44]

King Leopold has given up the Belgian Army. Sent *Some Tame Gazelle* to Curtis Brown [literary agents].[45]

First strawberries from the garden. The Germans are in Paris. Curtis Brown won't take *Some Tame Gazelle*.[46]

Undeterred she went on writing. Her 'Home Front' novel was written mostly in 1939, while the events it records were going on around her:

Church full of evacuees and some soldiers. Made notes for a war novel.[47]

Busy in the morning turning sheets sides to middle. Wrote quite a lot of my Home Front novel.[48]

She never finished this novel, nor one called *The Lumber Room*: 'After tea I did some writing or rather looking over a novel I started nearly three years ago. I may make something of it.'[49]

But she did complete a rough first draft of what she called her spy novel:

About 3:25 a.m. the sirens went! So off on my bike feeling rather foolish in my tin hat. I think I must write my spy novel.[50]

Did ironing and writing—the spy complications are very difficult.[51]

It is getting rather involved and I don't quite know what I am driving at—that's the worst of a plot.[52]

Writing I have done over 190 pages and really should be able to finish it now.[53]

She also wrote a short story called 'Goodbye Balkan Capital', which she sent to Penguin New Writing, though it was rejected.

In all these works she was increasing her powers of observation, looking at things in her own particular way. There are many passages of 'pure Pym' and some that she used, suitably revised, in her later novels. Above all, she was sharpening and enriching her style by the continuous practice of her craft.

In November 1941, when Barbara was 28, she noted in her diary, 'They are going to take all women of 20–30 from voluntary occupations'.[54] She had previously considered joining one of the women's services.

Thinking about whether to go into the W.A.A.F. Can't make up my mind what to do.[55]

I was altogether in a restless and unenviable state today, wondering whether I ought not to be in some job or one of the services for my own sake as well as for patriotic reasons.[56]

She applied for a job in the Censorship, which would involve censoring letters to and from neutral countries.

Doing Swedish and German. Had a letter from the Censors fixing appointment for two tests in languages.[57]

[In London] Wandered in Hill Street and was shocked at the desolation—and soldiers playing football in Eaton Square. Censorship interview. Very tired.[58]

In the evening studying German hard, trying to get a political vocabulary and practical in Deutsche Schrift which I couldn't do in the Censorship test.[59]

Most exhausting but enjoyable day, putting up new blackout etc. In the middle of it all came a wire from the Censorship offering me

a job in Bristol starting *Monday next*. I accepted. It will be lovely
to be with Poopa.[60]

So Barbara went to Bristol, where Hilary was working for
the BBC, and joined her at The Coppice, a large house on the
outskirts of the city, which they shared with several other
families. Barbara's life became different once again. From then
until the end of the war, she wrote no more fiction.

The period of 1939–41 which Barbara spent at home
provided a pause between the youthful excitements of Oxford
and the more hectic later war years. It gave Barbara a chance to
immerse herself in the sort of life that provided a background
for many of her heroines, even if they, like their creator,
eventually left it in order to pass on to other things. But
through this experience, the novelist acquired a grasp of the
fundamentals that ethos—practical, moral, almost stoical, yet
with a kind of lively frivolity—which would sustain her
through many vicissitudes.

Notes

All quotations are from Barbara Pym's Diaries, currently held by The
Bodleian Library, Oxford. The references cover four years, 1938–41 and
The Bodleian Library Reference Numbers are as follows:
1938: Pym, MS 104
1939: Pym, MS 105
1940: Pym, MS 106
1941: Pym, MS 107

1. 17 September 1941
2. 4 January 1938
3. 20 November 1939
4. 1 December 1939
5. 26 December 1939
6. 30 December 1939
7. 31 December 1939
8. 2 September 1939
9. 4 September 1939
10. 27 September 1939; 29 September 1939; 2 October 1939; 15 October
    1939
11. 30 September 1939
12. 15 September 1939
13. 13 October 1939

14. 21 April 1940
15. 29 April 1940
16. 16 June 1940
17. 17 June 1940
18. 19 June 1940; 29 June 1940
19. 20 December 1940
20. 15 April 1941
21. 7 May 1941
22. 18 July 1940
23. 4 February 1941
24. 19 February 1941; 5 February 1941
25. 15 December 1940
26. 6 January 1941
27. 8 March 1941
28. 25 January 1941
29. 26 May 1941
30. 16 October 1940; 17 October 1940
31. 4 January 1941
32. 10 January 1941
33. 13 January 1941
34. 30 January 1941
35. 13 February 1941
36. 25 August 1941
37. 11 October 1939
38. 1 July 1941
39. 23 March 1941
40. 15 August 1941
41. 10 February 1939
42. 22 December 1939
43. 10 April 1940
44. 25 April 1940
45. 28 May 1940
46. 14 June 1940; 15 June 1940
47. 1 October 1939
48. 9 October 1939
49. 24 January 1941
50. 26 August 1941
51. 22 September 1941
52. 9 October 1941
53. 28 October 1941
54. 3 November 1941
55. 25 July 1941
56. 13 September 1941
57. 22 November 1941
58. 26 November 1941
59. 29 November 1941
60. 9 December 1941

PART TWO: NEW APPROACHES

How does Barbara Pym regard men? This is an important question, since her heroines often seem obsessed with romantic love—most frequently with unrequited love. Her narrators tend to satirize men harshly. The following essays address the subject of Pym's bachelor characters and the related topic of her treatment of homosexuality. They reveal a narrative strategy which marginalizes the bachelor and makes him a figure of fun because of his immense self-absorption, a trait which renders him insensitive to those around him. Pym's heroines, by contrast, are often extremely sensitive to the expectations of others. Indeed, Pym's detachment and irony often challenge those characters who conform to the dominant culture, and draw the reader into complicity with the novels' heroines. Perhaps nowhere is the effect of Pym's subversive subtext so keenly felt as in relation to her narrators' outward deference to social expectations, matched by their inward criticism. At the same time, these challenges occur in the realm of private thought, where the reader and narrator join the heroines in their isolation. And although Pym's tolerance extends to homosexuals and even to 'straight' men, one detects in her work an undercurrent of contempt for the male sex, not least because they are able to thrive in this system.

Chapter 4

Text and the Single Man: The Bachelor in Pym's Dual-Voiced Narrative

LAURA L. DOAN

In *Excellent Women* the narrator, Mildred Lathbury, is startled by Mr Mallett's assumption that she, presumably one of those observant spinsters, would know who was moving into the building where she rents a flat. Mildred records this conversation as the novel opens: ' "Ah, you ladies! Always on the spot when there's something happening!" The voice belonged to Mr Mallett . . . and its roguish tone made me start guiltily, almost as if I had no right to be discovered outside my own front door' (*EW*, 5). Although Mildred is irritated by the intrusive insinuation, and in spite of her conviction that she has every right to wonder about her new neighbour, she responds not with sarcasm but with a tone of civility: ' "Well, yes, one usually does", I said, feeling rather annoyed at his presumption. "It is rather difficult not to know such things" ' (*EW*, 5). The irony here results from the tension that arises in the juxtaposition of the dutiful and subversive voice. Mildred's complex response to this unpleasant encounter, her annoyance with the question and her immediate guilty resignation to the charge, is typical of Pym's heroines. Mildred might wickedly contemplate a sharp retort of 'mind your own business' but she would, of course, refrain.

This episode is paradigmatic of a narrative strategy that calls for the continuous, simultaneous sounding of two narrative voices. On the surface, the reader is presented with a narrative voice fully compliant with normal social expectations—a voice politely civil even when answering an impudent, audacious query. Yet underneath this veneer of mild-mannered conformity, another voice speaks to challenge, even to ridicule, a social order that calls for the repression of unkind retorts. On this level, Mildred characterizes Mallett's remarks as roguish and pompous, but she internalizes her anger and irritation. These deeper feelings are revealed only to the reader. Most of Pym's characters are continually engaged in this quiet, civilized struggle which pits their individual needs against the larger set of social expectations. It is a rare occasion indeed when a Pym character freely pursues personal needs or desires without guilt. Yet when such incidents do occur, it is generally the bachelor—more than any other character type— who resists the constraints imposed by the dutiful voice. An examination of the bachelor's capacity to disrupt the dual-voiced narrative thus provides an important perspective on the way in which Pym's sexual ideology informs her narrative structure. But before we examine the implications of the single man's disruption of the narrative, we must first consider what sort of bachelor Pym presents.

The bachelor figure in Pym's novels is a curiously emasculated individual with many of the characteristics usually associated with spinsters. This lack of manliness emerges most clearly in the types of professions that Pym assigns her bachelors. Norman in *Quartet in Autumn*, for example, holds down a dreary and unimportant job in a nondescript London office. Even his own brother-in-law 'had always felt a sort of pitying contempt for [Norman], being so *unmanly* and working as a clerk in an office with middle-aged women' (*QA*, 13, emphasis mine). Similarly, in *Excellent Women* William Caldicote's job as a civil servant somewhere near Whitehall is dull and insignificant. Both men are characterized in their professions as diffident, subservient and retiring. For example, William's life revolves around the routine of feeding the pigeons that come to his office window punctually at quarter past three. When Mildred ventures to suggest that a change in such a routine might be pleasant on occasion, he replies peevishly, ' "They've moved me to a new office and I don't like it at all. Different pigeons come to the window" ' (*EW*, 71). William's drab and fussy disposition, here linked directly to his profession, leaves him an unlikely candidate for marriage. Although Mildred recognizes that William's sister, Dora, would like them to become engaged, she eventually comes to realize that 'William was not the kind of man to marry' (*EW*, 66).

In *Some Tame Gazelle*, Dr Nicholas Parnell continuously snoops around the library, enforcing rules and regulations. Parnell, 'small and bearded . . . not somehow . . . the kind of person one would marry', once seemed to promise significant contributions to scholarship; but these efforts are now all but forgotten (*STG*, 94). Although Parnell works in—indeed, he is the head of—a great university research library, his attention is wholly devoted to the less momentous task of ensuring the physical comfort of scholars using the library. His pressing duties apparently include worrying about the library heating system and dining facilities. Pym gently mocks Parnell's inflated sense of self-importance with a rhetorical question: 'For who can produce a really scholarly work when he is sitting shivering in a too heavy overcoat, struggling all the time against the temptation to go out and get himself a warming cup of coffee?' (*STG*, 82). Here an interrogatory tone works far more effectively than a stronger, more censorious comment to suggest the dubious nature of Parnell's own self-esteem. Pym uses both understatement and humour to belittle her bachelor.

Pym depicts the anthropologist's profession, like that of many bachelor occupations, as anti-social as well as strange and unnatural. In *An Unsuitable Attachment*, anthropologist Rupert Stonebird is trained professionally to do the sort of things that spinsters are expected to do naturally: to observe others carefully and with scientific detachment. 'Rupert was a quiet sort of person who disliked pushing himself forward and was therefore well fitted to observe the behaviour of others' (*UA*, 34). Rupert's diffident inclination to appear inconspicuous as well as his sporadic sense of self-effacement are both stereotypically spinsterish traits. When confronted with John and Ianthe's wedding at the end of the novel, Rupert instinctively separates himself from the ritual and resorts to an anthropologist's viewpoint: 'Although Ianthe's wedding was not at all like [those encountered in his African field work] . . . he was able to observe the proceedings with the same keen detachment as on those other occasions' (*UA*, 249).

Pym relentlessly exposes the bachelor's innumerable imperfections to the reader's scrutiny. Because he leads an incomplete life, the bachelor derives satisfaction in noting the things that can go wrong, in putting people down, in prying into the lives of others. For example, in *Crampton Hodnet* Edward Killigrew, described as a tall, middle-aged man with a fussy, petulant voice, lives with his mother and finds entertainment in spiteful bits of gossip about his co-workers. He even goes to the extreme of following an Oxford don, Francis Cleveland, and his student Barbara Bird, all the way from Oxford to London so that he can spy on their illicit love affair in order to repeat the titillating details to his mother over tea. 'He felt happier than he had felt for a long time. There had been nothing like this since that disgraceful affair of old Mr Pringle and the underground bookstore' (*CH*, 100). Later, when Francis discovers that his wife has been told about the affair, he thinks 'Of course all those gossiping North Oxford women were to blame [including] Edward Killigrew. You could lump him in with the women and never notice the difference' (*CH*, 194). Francis's suggestion that Edward could be '[lumped]. . . in with the women' emphasizes Killigrew's role as village gossip and encapsulates Pym's tactic of undermining the masculinity of the bachelor.

Thus Pym creates an unsympathetic portrayal by appropriating spinsterish qualities and embedding them into the character of the bachelor. Parnell's pettiness and Rupert Stonebird's quiet observation of others reflect stereotypically spinster-like attitudes towards life. William Caldicote's agitation and aggravation over minor details also seem spinsterish, as Mildred patiently notices when they have lunch together in a restaurant:

> He was in a fussy mood today, I could see, as he went rather petulantly through the menu. The liver would probably be overdone, the duck not enough done, the weather had been too mild for the celery to be good—it seemed as if there was really nothing we could eat. (*EW*, 67)

The bachelor's obsession with the trivial, suggested here by his finicky eating habits, exposes his shallowness and indicates how utterly oblivious he is to the mood or opinions of others. At a later point in the meal, Mildred observes how William refills his own wine glass but not hers.

Simone de Beauvoir writes that 'the advantage man enjoys, which makes itself felt from his childhood, is that his vocation as a human being in no way runs counter to his destiny. . . . He is not divided.'[1] Pym disputes this wholeness, which de Beauvoir claims for men, by presenting the bachelor as a character whose private life is at odds with, and is threatened by, his public career. He is often unable to reconcile the public and private spheres. When Pym introduces each of the four characters in *Quartet in Autumn* in the context of the public domain of the office, the men are described first and the women second. But when the characters return home, signalling a move from the external to the more intimate side of their lives, Pym suddenly and subtly switches the order and the women come first. While Pym establishes the domestic side of Marcia and Letty's lives in great detail (what they eat, the arrangement of their furniture, even the way in which their underwear is arranged in their dresser drawers), she glosses over the daily routine of the men. The reader knows only that Norman lives in a bed-sitter. Edwin's sphere is primarily that of the church, and again the reader sees him in this context but not in his house.

Pym's strategy to neglect the bachelor's private world relegates him to the margins because, in her view, he exists only within the context of his work. If, as Pym believes, the richness of life is in the daily routine of the private domain, the bachelor is disadvantaged, rather than privileged—a condition highlighted in those rare descriptions of his private life. Because the bachelor finds any personal exposure so distasteful and intrusive, the actual descriptions of bed-sitters or teas with mother are consistently overshadowed by his apparent discomfort. By essentially reversing the public/private dichotomy, the bachelor is in fact twice marginalized. The power base of the male—the public domain—is empty and impersonal, the least valued, while the private dimension is largely absent. Instead there is a silence, a gap.

Bachelors are often assigned professions that severely inhibit, even thwart, their relationships with the opposite sex

and with society at large. Thus while the librarian's preoccupation with trivialities leads to a debilitating self-
absorption, the anthropologist's obsession with esoteric topics
inhibits communication with the opposite sex. Consider, for
instance, Pym's characterization of the anthropologist Rupert
Stonebird in *An Unsuitable Attachment*, who is 'so ordinary-
looking that his very lack of distinction was in itself reassuring'
(*UA*, 14). Since Rupert finds conversation difficult, Penelope,
finding him unresponsive to her 'semi-flirtatious' looks, decides that 'it must be something to do with being an anthropologist . . . it seemed a dark mysterious profession, perhaps in a
way not quite manly, or not manly in the way she was used to'
(*UA*, 83). The sorts of subjects that interest Rupert, the
extra-marital relations of an obscure African tribe, for example, are difficult, inaccessible and uninteresting to the unin-
itiated. As a result, Rupert's attempt to explain a complicated
anthropological paper to Ianthe becomes not only an impossible task in itself but 'it was the kind of thing that could be, and
so often was, the stumbling block between men and women,
or, if a relationship had progressed through several stages, the
last straw' (*UA*, 213). Yet the irony of the bachelor's situation
is that the very job that emasculates him, and consequently
inhibits his interaction with women, remains the fixed focal
point of his life. His job is his primary interest and anyone
interacting with him must accept the centrality of such subjects
as card catalogues, library heating systems or the jural processes among the Ngumu.

The ultimate price the bachelor pays for a truncated life
focused solely on work is most clearly seen in *Quartet in
Autumn*, which describes the lives of four single people on the
brink of retirement. One of the women, Marcia, observes that
' "A woman can always find plenty to occupy her time. . . . It
isn't like a man retiring, you know. I have my house to see to" '
(*QA*, 108). The other female character of the quartet also
contemplates this predicament and concurs with Marcia's
conclusion: ' "A woman can always find plenty to occupy her
time"—that was the great thing. . . . It was men one felt sorry
for in retirement' (*QA*, 112). Paradoxically, while both
women express their belief that retirement for men is different
and difficult, even deserving of sympathy, the situation in the

novel is more complex. Letty and Norman exemplify characters who conform to this pattern, but the roles are somewhat reversed for Marcia and the widower Edwin. As an eccentric loner, Marcia's behaviour is consistently presented as deviant, while Edwin is a regular, if itinerant, church-goer. Rarely in one parish long enough to really fit in, Edwin is not part of a church community. In general, the men in Pym's fiction can barely be expected to cope in their retirement because they have failed to acquire either any outside interests or a network with which to connect. The spinster has her church, committees, neighbours and friends; the bachelor, once retired, rarely has any of these. By intentionally depriving the bachelor of interests that would enable him to establish relationships with others, Pym implies that his obsession with his work will become even more problematic upon retirement because the fundamental emptiness and aimlessness of his life will become all too apparent.

Pym's bachelors fall roughly into two categories. The first are confirmed bachelors who remain single by choice because they are convinced that it is a more desirable state. The second group consists of single men who are available for marriage and are not single by choice. The first group often includes men who seem to be more effeminate and prissy, traits often associated with homosexuals. Edward Killigrew in *Crampton Hodnet*, who in middle age lives at home with his mother and who thrives on gossip, is typical of this kind of bachelor. Adam Prince in *A Few Green Leaves* is another example. His career as a restaurant reviewer somehow sets him apart from ordinary men. A former Church of England clergyman, Adam has given up the worship of God for the worship of food. His preoccupation with restaurants and menus culminates in a debilitating perfectionism. Adam reacts with exasperation

> at seeing a bottle of wine being warmed up ('chambréed') on a storage heater, or being offered vinegary bottled mayonnaise instead of home-made, or sliced bread or processed cheese, or . . . the use of tea-bags—that seemed to upset him quite unreasonably. (*FGL*, 208)

Even as a clergyman, he had been more concerned with the superficial aspects of his work, such as the arrangement of flowers and the selection of wines, than in the running of the parish. Although he is one of the few eligible single men in the village, it is obvious to everyone, including Isabel who is looking for a potential husband for her daughter, that Adam is not a marrying man. In Adam's view, sex is something distasteful: when he inadvertently comes across two lovers kissing in the woods, he turns away from the upsetting sight and returns home for a consoling cup of Lapsang tea.

Another excellent specimen of the so-called confirmed bachelor in Pym's fiction is the middle-aged librarian Mervyn Cantrell in *An Unsuitable Attachment*. Mervyn is very possibly one of the nastiest characters in the Pym canon, a man whose very description suggests an unpleasant nature: he is 'a tall thin irritable-looking man' (*UA*, 26). Like Nicholas Parnell, Mervyn's career has taken a downward swing and he has never been able to achieve the sort of distinguished position that he desired. Mervyn's petty obsession with trivial details in the post which he currently holds functions as a palliative for his failure in more important matters. In spite of his irascible and petulant manner, co-worker Ianthe Broome feels that she ought to treat him with compassion. When Mervyn revels in the mistakes of others, rather than censure his triumphant gloating, Ianthe sadly reflects:

> Poor Mervyn, she knew that she ought to feel sorry for him, living with his disagreeable old mother . . . disappointed at not having got a job in one of the University libraries, unable to find staff accurate enough to appreciate the niceties of setting out a bibliographical entry correctly, with it seemed few friends of either sex, unable to eat restaurant food—really, the list seemed endless when one thought about it. (*UA*, 27–8)

As with other bachelors, Mervyn is relegated to the extreme margins of the text. His private life is described in only enough detail to reinforce the impression that he is a homosexual. His life with, and devotion to, his mother is mentioned, but Pym never explores his private life further in the novel.

Although ostensibly a confirmed bachelor, Mervyn becomes quite interested in Ianthe, or more precisely, in her 'lovely' antiques. When three bachelors descend on Ianthe's house, 'John and Rupert [sit] down rather stiffly, not quite liking to roam about the room appraising the furniture and objects, as Mervyn was doing' (*UA*, 68). Oblivious that his inquisitiveness embarrasses the others, Mervyn abandons common courtesy and pursues his transparent objective: to acquire Ianthe's house and personal belongings. For Mervyn, marriage is a union of possessions, an arrangement of convenience. He proposes to her in these terms: ' "there's marriage and marriage, if you see what I mean . . . We get on well together . . . and we've many interests in common, after all . . . we both like nice furniture" ' (*UA*, 203). Mervyn's idea of marriage does not entail romantic love (it rarely does for Pym's men). In Pym's depiction of Mervyn we find a relentless critique of a bachelor whose selfish motives are blatant and repulsive.

The second type of bachelor, the single man available for marriage, is often reduced to the status of an object in Pym's novels. It is not the persona of the bachelor himself which is important; his significance is determined almost exclusively on the basis of his eligibility. Because Pym aggrandizes this type of bachelor, he can become a desirable object around which the plot revolves. This is precisely the case with Rupert in *An Unsuitable Attachment*, whom both Sophia and Penelope regard not as a person but as an object to acquire. Sophia admits that the single man is intriguing because he 'probably inspires wider and wilder speculation than a single woman . . . his unmarried state is in itself more interesting than a woman's unmarriedness' (*UA*, 248). What Sophia refers to here is not the individual himself, who is essentially a non-entity in this scheme, but simply the bachelor's eligibility. Sophia carefully surveys Rupert's habits throughout the novel in the hope of manoeuvring her sister Penelope into a better position to catch him.

The most sought after figure among this group of eligible bachelors is the vicar. This individual is perhaps one of the most interesting of Pym's single men because, inasmuch as his profession is his life, theoretically the public and the private should merge. These high social expectations put the vicar in an exceptionally awkward position: his call to serve others stands in conflict with his natural masculine self-absorption.

He has trouble establishing the kind of networks which the spinsters in his parish seem to acquire so easily. Mark Ainger, the married vicar in *An Unsuitable Attachment*, remains a bachelor by temperament in spite of his unsuitable marriage with Sophia. His remote character, a quality referred to often by the narrator, renders him an ineffectual husband and clergyman. Though kind and courteous, Mark is not 'particularly interested in human beings', a quality which he tries to overcome only because 'he feels he ought to' (*UA*, 17, 84). Mark's inability or failure to meet the demands of his vocation means that he, like other vicars, has more room to fall than other men.

This difficulty in relating to parishioners is compounded for clergymen who are unmarried. As a result of the unhealthy self-absorption, the unmarried vicar is frequently ill at ease with his parishioners, socially and embarrassingly out of touch with their needs. He is also more than willing to accept the care of adoring female parishioners and the efforts of spinsters in his parish. Thus a clergyman such as Neville Forbes in *No Fond Return of Love* is gracious to the point of being unctuous, and accepts devotion from the women in his church as his due. As a man of the church, the bachelor-vicar faces the awkward and disconcerting task of deciding how to reconcile sexuality and celibacy. At times the two seem irreconcilable, as Julian Malory in *Excellent Women* suggests in complaining about his own situation: ' "I suppose I am not to be considered as a normal man . . . and yet I do have these manly feelings" ' (*EW*, 42). Both Julian's sister, Winifred, and Mildred Lathbury repeatedly state that Julian is not the marrying kind, but other characters in the novel persistently push Mildred towards him. Julian becomes positively pompous in his laboured apologies to Mildred for having preferred another to her, and this shows his innate assumption that he is consummately eligible.

The arrogance that attends the bachelor's awareness of his eligibility can lead to a complicated game of shifting alliances for the vicar, who is inclined to take advantage of his situation. The Reverend David Lydell in *Quartet in Autumn* is a most complacent object of adoration by women of the parish. Conscious only of his own desires and happiness, he is content to linger on after sherry, to receive a dinner invitation and to allow the women of the house to fuss over him. After a lengthy engagement to one of the women, Marjorie, he does not hesitate to call off the wedding and to succumb to the identical attention of another woman in the village (an action that suggests the arrangement of marriage partners is arbitrary and interchangeable). In a similar way, Stephen Latimer in *Cramp-ton Hodnet* proposes to one woman because it seem convenient. When he is refused, he simply looks for a potential bride elsewhere. Stephen's immodest opinion of himself is clearly evident when he ponders the marriage question:

> He was a man of private means, good-looking and charming. It was obvious that he could never expect to have much peace until he was safely married. Besides, there was something comforting about the idea of having a wife, a helpmeet, somebody who would keep the others off and minister to his needs. (*CH*, 63–4)

Rupert Stonebird, in *An Unsuitable Attachment*, falls somewhere between the confirmed and the reluctant bachelor. As mentioned earlier, he is seen as an eligible husband by Penelope, but he finds certain aspects of the single life appealing. In fact, Rupert's subtlety in dealing with women is potentially more insidious and dangerous because his motives are more difficult to read. Rupert also proposes to Ianthe, and like Mervyn, his reaction to her rejection is one of incredulity—a characteristic response from Pym's bachelors. When Ianthe reveals that she loves another, we are told that 'the effect of this flat statement was devastating, for it was the last thing Rupert had expected' (*UA*, 217). The narrator gives no indication that Rupert is in any way sensitive to Ianthe's 'agitation'; the reader is only informed that he himself feels 'foolish'. The bachelor's inability to interact with others is clearly delineated in Rupert's response to Ianthe. When Ianthe begins to cry, a situation that Rupert has no intention of dealing with, he abruptly removes her from his house and escorts her back across the street.

Pym implies that from the bachelor's point of view, to be refused in marriage is the ultimate insult. Since bachelors feel somehow privileged in their single status, when they elect to marry, they believe that a woman should feel honoured. Everything, especially a marriage proposal, is confidently expected to go their way. The irony again is that since the bachelor is so self-absorbed, he fails to understand that being married to him might not, in fact, be so appealing. The bachelor's flawed psychological apparatus can often lead to a rebuff, as in the case of Rupert and Ianthe. Because the bachelor rarely considers the feelings of other people, he is surprisingly unsophisticated in his personal relationships and, as a result, constantly caught off-guard by their reactions. It is perhaps only his bemused naïveté that saves him from seeming completely pathetic in the eyes of the reader.

Earlier I suggested that Pym's dual-voiced narrative is a device that enables her characters to challenge and subvert prevailing social expectations. Yet this device is missing for the bachelor; an absence seen, for instance, in Mervyn's reaction to Ianthe's rejection of his marriage proposal in *An Unsuitable Attachment*. Mervyn's inner thoughts are completely absent from the text even though he gives full vent to his umbrage that Ianthe would have the audacity to say no: ' "And why not, might I ask?" he said petulantly, almost nastily' (*UA*, 203). The silence in the narrative surrounding Mervyn's private thoughts implies two things. One is that he operates on such a superficial level that he is not even sure what his own feelings are. The other is that he is incapable of any sort of human feeling for another person, either compassion or love. Mervyn's absence of emotion stands in sharp contrast to the immense amount of information Pym provides concerning Ianthe's response. Ianthe can only articulate her amazement about the proposal if she does so instinctively and without thinking: ' "But I couldn't marry you!" she burst out' (*UA*, 203). Within seconds, however, she collects herself and re-gains her self-control. In a state of composure, any expression of her true feelings is out of the question, so 'Ianthe sat in a dismayed silence' (*UA*, 203). Within the space of a few brief moments, Ianthe has experienced a full range of emotions, from outrage to polite restraint. But during the same brief period, the description of Mervyn is restricted to his bare statements and the tone in which they are delivered.

Later Mervyn repairs to his favourite restaurant to lick his wounds, as if culinary compensation would provide sufficient reparation. Here the narrator first dangles the possibility of emotion, then retracts it immediately: '[the meal] had done a good deal to restore his spirits and heal his wounded pride, if it had been wounded' (*UA*, 238). With this qualification, Pym thoroughly negates any possibility of authentic feeling on Mervyn's part, even that of a suitor's wounded pride. Although his plans to marry Ianthe are hopeless, Mervyn's jealousy and pettiness drive him to retaliate against her by casting aspersions on John, her future husband. Yet the last time Mervyn appears in the narrative, he brags to two other bachelors that ' "if it hadn't been for me we shouldn't be here at her wedding today" ' (*UA*, 252). Throughout these events, Mervyn's actions and statements are firmly restricted to the surface; a second voice never emerges to challenge surface appearances or impressions. There is no suggestion that Mervyn considers Ianthe's feelings for an instant; she exists simply as a metonym for her possessions. The reader must conclude that Mervyn's exterior behaviour is the manifestation of his innermost thoughts: selfish and self-serving. This is strikingly different in comparison with Ianthe's dual reaction; her dismayed silence is only a veneer for her expression of outrage at Mervyn's suggestion of marriage.

When Pym reveals the innermost thoughts of the characters in *Quartet in Autumn*, it is to separate the insensitive and unfeeling bachelor from the dutiful widower and spinsters who share his office. After Letty and Marcia retire, it is Edwin, not Norman, who arranges a lunchtime reunion: 'it had been his idea to invite Letty and Marcia to lunch. His conscience had been nagging at him and in the end he had written to them' (*QA*, 127). Edwin's sense of obligation is so unusual for a male character in Pym's fiction that some sort of justification must be found for his action. A nagging conscience is probably the result of two factors that distinguish Edwin from Norman: he is a church-goer and a widower. Norman would not think to invite the ladies to lunch because, as a bachelor, he is not in the habit of performing selfless deeds. (He does, of course, visit his brother-in-law Ken in hospital, out of some sense of family loyalty, but for the most part Norman enjoys his misanthropic isolation.)

Once the four are reunited, Norman fails to rise to the
occasion and remains his usual unpleasant self. Marcia's
emaciated and strange appearance at the luncheon evokes a
different response from all three:

> Edwin, who was not particularly observant, did realise that
> [Marcia] was wearing an odd assortment of garments but did not
> think she looked much different from usual. Norman thought,
> poor old girl, obviously going round the bend. Letty, as a clothes-
> conscious woman, was appalled—that anyone could get to the
> stage of caring so little about her appearance, of not even noticing
> how she looked, made her profoundly uneasy and almost
> conscience-stricken, as if *she* ought to have done something more
> about Marcia in her retirement. (*QA*, 129–30)

Here the narrator allows a rare glimpse into the inner thoughts
of a bachelor, and not surprisingly, he displays little concern
for the well-being of another. Norman merely attributes the
dramatic change in Marcia's appearance to her dubious mental state—a pitiless and dispassionate appraisal that compares
unfavourably with Edwin's atypical sartorial observation and
Letty's complex response of shock and guilt. Norman even
goes so far as to make an impolite comment to Marcia: ' "You
look as if you could do with a square meal", said Norman
bluntly' (*QA*, 130). Pym credits the widower for the act of
observing and informs the reader that such behaviour is not
the norm. The spinster, as usual, is already worrying that she
has not done enough and quickly reviews her past behaviour
critically: 'now [Letty] was made to feel ashamed because she
felt embarrassed at the idea of sitting . . . with Marcia' (*QA*,
130). There is no hint, however, that Norman as a bachelor
feels any responsibility for Marcia. In pronouncing her men-
tally unbalanced, he absolves himself from any sense of duty
towards her.

The bachelor's absence from the dual-voiced narrative has
important implications because it functions as a device for
delineating the male from the female voice and acts as a
commentary on the bachelor's self-interest. Implicit in the
bachelor's exclusion from the dual-voiced narrative is the
assumption that he cannot experience guilt and does not
possess a sense of duty. The mechanism of the dual voices,

therefore, is unnecessary. The case of Pym's spinster, on the other hand, is entirely different. She cannot choose between personal needs or social demands. To reject or ignore the latter would result in guilt, and so Pym provides the spinster with a mechanism to subvert the social order while continuing to function within it. Her inner thoughts challenge and ridicule the dominant order, allowing for a cathartic release. Thus when Ianthe in *An Unsuitable Attachment* realizes that her plans for a quiet evening alone conflict with a church meeting, there is no question as to what she will decide. Her subversive voice of wilful rebellion will allow her to imagine 'rather selfishly . . . a quiet evening at home surrounded by familiar objects, perhaps reading or listening to a concert on the wireless', but the other voice will reinforce her sense of obligation (*UA*, 50–1). Her reckless impulses must be brought under control. Ianthe herself is fully aware that the bachelor does not have to heed the dutiful voice; ' "I shouldn't think [Rupert will] be there. Men don't usually take much part in these things" ' (*UA*, 51). For the bachelor, the dutiful voice is non-existent. Whereas Penelope wonders if Rupert will attend the meeting, Ianthe knows he will not. The younger, less experienced woman is left wondering 'surely it was [Rupert's] duty to be?' (*UA*, 51).

Rupert is one of the more ambiguous bachelors in Pym's fiction, and a complete disregard for duty comes less easily to him than it would to someone like Mervyn. Since, as I have suggested earlier, Pym appropriates spinsterish traits and qualities in order to draw connections between the spinster and the anthropologist, Rupert's character is an unusual amalgam. His possession of both male and female traits results in a confused identity manifested in the reawakening of his conscience, a condition that leaves him uncomfortable and perplexed. Normally the question of whether or not to attend the church bazaar, for instance, would not even present itself for consideration; but lately a strange new sense of duty had been pricking his conscience:

It was disquieting . . . the way he seemed to have to make these excuses to himself, as if his conscience which he had, so he thought at the age of sixteen, successfully buried, had suddenly

reawakened to plague him, not about the fundamentals of belief
and morality but about such comparative trivialities as whether or
not one should attend the church bazaar. (*UA*, 67)

The very fact that Rupert finds the whole experience 'disquieting' is evidence enough to suggest that male feelings of duty or
obligation are out of the ordinary. He has difficulty even
understanding how such an unusual state of affairs has
transpired.

At the end of the novel, Rupert is given the chance to
perform another thankless and unselfish task, and not surprisingly, he is ambivalent about carrying it out. As Ianthe and
John's wedding approaches, Rupert 'had thought for a time
that he ought to offer to put John up for the wedding and had
seriously considered that it might be his duty' (*UA*, 249). Once
again, it is extraordinary that Rupert considers the possibility
of performing a gracious and gratuitous act. Moreover, Pym
suggests that Rupert might even imagine such a gesture as his
duty. But, as with the church bazaar episode earlier, procras-
tination allows him to avert actually having to carry out an
unpleasant task. Rupert differs significantly from Mervyn,
who would not contemplate such a pointless gesture, but he is
nevertheless incapable of such a deed. This is because, as a bachelor, Rupert is not subject to the voice that plagues Ianthe and
her female counterparts. The sense of duty and obligation is
absent. There are no clues in the narrative to suggest that
Rupert's conscience could be so moved that he would feel
compelled to offer accommodation: 'there was a certain delicacy about the situation, and while he was reflecting Sister
Dew had offered, "come to the rescue", as she put it' (*UA*,
249). Ironically, in Pym's novels 'coming to the rescue' is an
act of chivalry far more suited to women than to bachelors.

Pym suspends the dual-voiced narrative for the bachelor in
order to delineate the chasm that exists between the conscien-
tiousness of men and women. The dichotomy between male
selfishness and female guilt, a major facet of Pym's sexual
ideology, is particularly evident when Pym uses first-person
narration. In *Excellent Women*, the female narrator's voice of
duty and guilt is often juxtaposed with the bachelor's selfish
demands on her. An example of this occurs when Everard
Bone rings Mildred Lathbury to ask if she would be interested

in coming over to cook his dinner. Although she struggles to control her feelings, Mildred's initial response, one of suspicion and unease, is not held in check and she complains, 'I had not wanted to see Everard Bone and the idea of having to cook his evening meal for him was more than I could bear at this moment' (*EW*, 219). But the very next sentence demonstrates that, although such inner feelings might be expressed to the reader, the dutiful voice is ineluctable: 'And yet the thought of him alone with his meat and his cookery book was unbearable too' (*EW*, 219–20). Mildred cannot hope to reconcile these conflicting feelings. While the thought of Everard's presence and the thought of cooking his meal are equally intolerable, Mildred cannot simply dismiss the offer without agonizing over the dilemma. Her assessment of the situation is worth quoting at length because it illustrates her immense capacity for guilt:

> He would turn to the section on meat. He would read that beef or mutton should be cooked for so many minutes per pound and so many over. He would weigh the little joint, if he had scales. He would then puzzle over the heat of the oven, turning it on and standing over it, watching the thermometer go up . . . I should have been nearly in tears at this point if I had not pulled myself together and reminded myself that Everard Bone was a very capable sort of person whose life was always very well arranged. He would be quite equal to cooking a joint. Men are not nearly so helpless and pathetic as we sometimes like to imagine them. (*EW*, 220)

Mildred seems to renounce any responsibility for Everard only to be finally overcome by a guilty conscience. With her quiet evening alone absolutely destroyed, she pays a visit to the vicarage 'to see if there was anything [she] could do there' (*EW*, 220). Mildred concludes that Everard has probably already invited someone else around to dinner. Whatever Everard did in fact decide to do is never revealed to Mildred or to the reader. Once again, the entire spectrum of a woman's emotions is exposed, while the bachelor remains taciturn. When Mildred declines Everard's offer, his 'flat and noncommittal' response is characteristically terse: ' "Oh, I'm sorry . . . Perhaps some other time?" ' (*EW*, 218–19).

Pym's bachelor character is separated from other men sing-
led out for special treatment. He is the least sympathetic of
Pym's characters: embittered, disgruntled, vulnerable, pathetic, petty, cynical, ambitious and selfish. While other characters may embody some of these traits from time to time, the
bachelor is far more likely to possess an inordinate number of
unpleasant qualities. Why? In Pym's view the bachelor possesses too much freedom. This total lack of responsibility to
anyone other than himself is, in a sense, his downfall. The
bachelor is under no obligation to alter his behaviour for
anyone, particularly for any woman. Married men, on the
other hand, must defer on occasion to the needs of others,
even if it is only to their wives. Because bachelors are absolutely free of the constraints and restrictions imposed by marriage, they constitute a special category of males in Pym's
fiction.

While the dominant social order privileges the bachelor, on
the deepest level of the narrative Pym exempts the bachelor
from normal social obligations and relegates him to a marginal
position. According to the social order, a bachelor is to be
envied for his autonomy. The bachelor is regarded as self-
sufficient, confident, resolute and self-possessed. Pym offers
the reader an alternative view of the bachelor by subverting the
dominant view. For Pym, the bachelor should be pitied because he is the most divided and divisive character. He is
doubly excluded from the dual-voiced narrative structure
because he has only one voice and no private life in which to
fully reveal himself. The bachelor's autonomy is shown as a
burden rather than as enviable, because he is lonely and
unfulfilled. This contrasts sharply with Pym's depiction of the
joyous autonomy of the spinster, who is not tied to serving a
man; the bachelor is only free from the responsibilities that
come from being attached to a female. The wide and wild
speculation that Sophia in *An Unsuitable Attachment* believes
to be engendered by the bachelor is emblematic of Pym's
subversive narrative strategy. By exempting the bachelor from
the dual-voiced narrative, Pym invents a wide and wild
strategy that undermines the patriarchy.

Note

1. Simone de Beauvoir, *The Second Sex* (1952), trans. H.M. Parshley, New York: Vintage, 1974, p. 758.

Chapter 5

Barbara Pym's Subversive Subtext: Private Irony and Shared Detachment

BARBARA BOWMAN

One of the troubling questions I have often asked myself about Barbara Pym's novels is 'Why have I always assumed that her narrator is a woman?' Do we automatically assume that the narrator is a woman if the author is? For instance, do we hear Jane Austen's narrator as the voice of a woman and Henry James's narrator as that of a man? Are we projecting our expectations as readers onto the writer's voice? While the case of Barbara Pym's fiction may not exemplify all such cases, some recurrent patterns in the way her narrators and heroines think and speak convince me that the narrators in her novels adopt points of view resembling those of her heroines and, furthermore, that her heroines think and speak in ways characteristic of women when they adopt a subordinate role. Readers of her novels, then, are not simply projecting their own expectations on that narrative voice, though they are, of course, participating in the way Pym defines a 'woman's' voice.

In *Excellent Women* this interaction between the reader and the text is somewhat simplified because Pym has chosen to use first-person narration: her narrator and heroine share a voice. (Only occasionally do the narrator's and heroine's voices diverge, but, even when they do, the two voices express similar sentiments.) Pym's heroine in *Excellent Women*, Mildred Lathbury, often outwardly advocates conventional behaviour while carrying on an elaborately layered dialogue with herself that subverts the conventional. When Mildred first meets Helena Napier, for instance, we see her questioning her own conventional notions of sexual roles. Helena says, 'Rocking-

82

ham does most of the cooking when we're together . . . I'm
really too busy to do much' (*EW*, 9). Mildred thinks out the
implications of this statement, beginning with a conventional
response but inverting it with an ironic observation:

> Surely wives shouldn't be too busy to cook for their husbands? I
> thought in astonishment, taking a thick piece of bread and jam
> from the plate offered to me. But perhaps Rockingham with his
> love of Victoriana also enjoyed cooking, for I had observed that
> men did not usually do things unless they liked doing them. (*EW*,
> 9)

Two characteristic linguistic patterns are present in this passage. First, the non-restrictive participial phrase which deflates
the heroine's automatic conventional response, 'taking a thick
piece of bread and jam from the plate'.[1] This action shows
Mildred not averse to others providing her with a generous tea
(she herself is, in other words, somewhat excluded from the
'giver' stereotype of women, 'wives who shouldn't be too busy
to cook for their husbands'). Second, the inversion starting
with 'but perhaps' concludes with the subversive observation
that men don't do things 'unless they [like] doing them'.

In this passage, the narrator's voice is somewhat disting-
uishable from the heroine's, though they arrive at similar
conclusions. I would attribute the participial phrase to the
narrator, who recognizes Mildred's complicity in Helena's
choice not to cook *a moment before* the inversion takes place
in Mildred's thinking. Even though the first-person point of
view would seem to disguise any distinction between a narrator's voice and the heroine's, the innocence with which Mildred reports 'taking a thick piece of bread' allows a somewhat
more complex layering of the heroine's response. For an
instant, the reader and the narrator share an irony of which
Mildred is unaware. This distance between the narrator and
the heroine disappears when Mildred inverts her first conventional response and implicitly decides for Helena's unconventional point of view (not to cook for her husband).

Mildred's means of expressing this point of view, 'I had
observed that men did not usually do things unless they liked
doing them', does align her firmly with the narrator and the

reader, because this declaration recalls the paradigmatic sort of irony present in Austen's novels, as for instance in the opening line of *Pride and Prejudice*: 'It is a truth universally acknowledged that a single man in possession of a good fortune must be in want of a wife.'[2] Both declarations are ironic (though the irony functions differently), and both exploit their irony by being couched as maxims.[3] The complexity of Austen's irony resides in the narrator's voice as it collides with the reader's recognition of the statement's untruth and its depiction of a useful social façade. Pym's irony uses some of the assumptions behind Austen's irony: (1) that the narrator and the reader's knowledge and points of view correspond, and (2) that the heroine will be initiated into this alignment of narrator and reader. And yet Pym's use of the maxim here emphasizes the heroine's dynamic discovery of *the truth* by delaying and thus dramatizing it. The maxim, unlike Austen's use of it in this case, expresses the process of discovering that truth: and the narrator, the reader, and the heroine share the delight of that discovery.

For those not gently obsessed by Barbara Pym's fiction, it may sound odd to speak of her heroines as subversive, since they are hardly radicals who protest loudly against the dominant culture's expectations. Still, I maintain that on the miniaturized scale of the novel of manners, which examines the intricacies of how men and women think and act, such a protest is indeed taking place. Within the world of Anglican parishes, jumble sales, ritualistic teas, and lectures at anthropological societies, Mildred in *Excellent Women* subverts the dominant culture's expectations and constructs an alternate system of linguistic codes marked by a keen sense of the ridiculous. At the same time, her subversion undermines these expectations rather than overthrowing them. Indeed, Mildred sometimes surprises herself when she subverts a convention. During the meeting to organize the St Mary's Christmas bazaar, for instance, she suggests to the other members of the church committee that they might forego having tea, which leads her to consider the far-reaching implications of this suggestion: 'I began to realize that my question had struck at something deep and fundamental. It was the kind of question that starts a landslide in the mind' (*EW*, 227).

Pym's heroines and narrators are not overtly feminist in the
sense that they set out to overthrow male domination, but they
do dramatize the heroine's perception of the discrepancy
between her own and the dominant culture's assumptions,
whether the dominant culture is represented by a male or by a
group of men and women. In the case of the church committee
which Mildred faces in the example above, more women than
men are engaged in upholding the dominant culture's ritualistic assumptions. But when a character's point of view is
aligned with the narrator's, that character is almost always
female, as in the case of Jessie Morrow in *Jane and Prudence*
and in *Crampton Hodnet*, Jane Cleveland in *Jane and Prudence*, Catherine Oliphant in *Less than Angels*, and Belinda
Bede in *Some Tame Gazelle*. And while women associated
with the dominant culture, like Miss Doggett in *Jane and
Prudence*, are often the butts of Pym's irony, a more familiar
situation—in these novels especially—poses the heroine's
perception of the discrepancy between her own and the dominant culture's assumptions against a male character's lack of
perception. Pym's male characters tend to be extremely complacent and self-satisfied.[4] In *Excellent Women*, Mildred says
to Winifred, the rector's sister, ' "don't you think men sometimes leave difficulties to be solved by other people or to solve
themselves?" ' (*EW*, 206).

Pym's fiction offers no programmatic hope that the relation
of dominants to subordinates might change, though it does
suggest that subordinates receive certain compensations for
their inferior status; the greatest of these is a superior power to
perceive and judge those around them. Thus in *Excellent
Women*, when Julian Malory discovers his mistake in becoming engaged to Mrs Gray, Mildred thinks, 'She was certainly
very pretty . . . but I did not say it. I could not add to the
burden of his humiliation by pointing out that he may have
been taken in, like so many men before him, by a pretty face'
(*EW*, 211). Of course, one of the disadvantages of being a
subordinate is the inability ever to savour triumph
wholeheartedly. Because Pym's heroines do not define their
perceptions in competition with others, Mildred cannot react
to Julian in a simple 'I told you so. Ha!' sort of way. As a
subordinate, her role is still to some extent defined by the

member of the dominant group. She enjoys the rightness of her judgement in silence to protect the rector from fully recognizing his own stupidity and conventionality. A similar doubleness is apparent in the meeting of Mildred and Everard Bone after a long period of separation:

> 'Are you going to have lunch? We may as well have it together.'
> 'Yes, I was going to', I said, and told him where I had thought of going.
> 'Oh, we can't go there', he said impatiently, so of course we went to a restaurant of his choice near the premises of the Learned Society.
> Naturally the meal did not come up to my expectations, though the food was very good. I found myself wondering how I could have wanted so much to see him again, and I was embarrassed at the remembrance of my imaginings of him, alone and ill in his flat with nobody to look after him. Nothing more unlikely could possibly be imagined (*EW*, 240–1)

The phrases 'of course' and 'Naturally' mark the two stages in the heroine's inversion. The first establishes the dominant culture's assumptions that the woman will follow the man's lead and that she will suppress her own idea. The second triggers the inversion, especially the heroine's complex judgement that their interaction was not satisfactory.

Pym's heroine/narrator here is not, however, an idealogue, for she barely accuses the male character. She admits, in fact, that 'the food was good'. What follows that admission, which effectively shifts the register of the analysis from the material to the emotional, is a self-examination by the heroine rather than a harshly judgemental analysis of Everard Bone's unconsciously overbearing manner. But the latter is also implicit in the former, even though it is unstated. It does not need to be stated. By castigating herself for bothering to worry about Everard, Mildred tries to cure herself of her own subordination—the habit of protecting the dominant male from knowing his own ineptness. This painful result of Pym's irony might be seen as a first step towards feminism—as the initial retraining of the subordinate to see the bankruptcy of her own habitual roles.

The subtlety and painfulness of Pym's irony are bound up

with its peculiar 'femaleness'. I use that noun advisedly since I do not see it as excluding the experience of men,[5] but by it I am describing the experience of subordination rather than of domination, especially as this experience has been described by Jean Baker Miller in *Toward a New Psychology of Women*.[6] The heroine's perception of ironic discrepancy in *Excellent Women* embodies many of the psychological patterns (but now in a linguistic format) so characteristic of women:

(1) Mildred recognizes, for instance, that she has been assigned 'acceptable roles'[7] of 'tea-maker in a crisis' and 'parish excellent woman who wants to marry the vicar' and 'index compiler for the scholarly man' by the dominant culture. Her response before this stereotyping is often resignation, for she finds she can't convince others that she does not resemble their notions of her. The woman who has joined the dominant culture as an anthropologist in *Excellent Women*, Helena Napier, is as guilty of stereotyping Mildred in this way as any of the men.

(2) What becomes more disturbing to the reader (and probably makes the enjoyment of Mildred's irony difficult for some readers) is Mildred's struggle with, and sometimes failure to struggle with, those 'psychological characteristics that are pleasing to the dominant group',[8] in other words, her self-deprecation, her lack of certainty and her tendency to be inconsistent. Pym shows us the traits of a subordinate from two angles, though she favours the interior perspective of her heroine. Viewed from the outside as a man might view a woman, Mildred looks inconsistent, whereas from her own perspective her inversions suggest a dynamically process-orientated self-definition. Still, she is in danger of becoming Everard Bone's indexer and proofreader at the end of the novel as a result of her flexibility despite her successful resistance to taking in Winifred as a roommate. (Is it one of Pym's bleaker ironies that Mildred is reported to have married Everard in *Less than Angels*, I wonder?)

(3) Mildred's intelligence and assertiveness are hidden from the males in the novel.[9] We hear about her ironic perceptions as thoughts reported through her first-person narration. She

knows these traits would shock the complacent and sometimes pompous men in the story: Julian Malory, Rocky Napier, William Caldicote and Everard Bone. She consequently enjoys her ironic perceptions privately, though the community that shares these ironies consists of the narrator Mildred and the reader. It is a privileged community—privileged by self-knowledge and understanding of others, their faults and worth—but the cost of this privilege is a sometimes oppressive social inferiority. I often feel this inferiority as a darkness of tone lurking behind the heroine's irony or wit. When it emerges more fully, as in Pym's later novels, *Quartet in Autumn* and *The Sweet Dove Died*, it evolves into fully-felt despair.

(4) Self-knowledge when it includes self-criticism is a characteristic trait of Pym's heroines.[10] In contrast, the male characters in Pym's novels fit into a pattern of rarely knowing their effect on others, knowing even less about the women around them, and avoiding most of the subtleties of their interaction with others of either sex. Pym opens up those areas of knowledge based on self-criticism through her heroines and narrators, and she does so dynamically: her heroines don't just *know* themselves or others automatically; they have to work at attaining those skills. A large part of the discomfort to the reader of Pym's novels is the heroine's frequent failures and her admissions of failure.

Pym, then, puts us, the readers, in an uncomfortably subordinate position when we listen to Mildred's first-person narration. We experience much of what women and other subordinates experience in a dominant culture:

(1) Mildred feels *guilty* when she feels that she is *not giving* enough, even though she discovers that Everard Bone, for instance, did not need her to cook his meat.[11] Still, she is a somewhat unusual female character since she knows that she needs to be self-protective about being drawn into giving roles. She evades both Winifred's plea for help and Julian's tentative proposal.

(2) All of the women in Pym's novels suffer from the assumption that their work is unworthy because it is defined as service rather than as inner-directed 'pursuit of their own goals'.[12]

Mildred in *Excellent Women* is triply humbled because she works only part-time for a Society for Distressed Gentlewomen. Her perception of her job's inferiority has three causes: it is a service for others; it is only part-time; and it serves women.

(3) Pym's heroines confront change in themselves and others.[13] That means that they confront others seriously enough to be moved and even slightly redefined by them. The permeable ego of these heroines is not a comfortable fictional model for many readers.[14] Mildred certainly tries to consolidate her identity, as when she self-consciously speaks of herself as 'spinsterish' (*EW*, 20); but not long after she accepts this convenient label for herself, it becomes too painful, as when she observes, 'I felt more than usually spinsterish and useless. Mrs Napier must be hard up for friends if she could find nobody better than me to confide in, I thought' (*EW*, 28).

(4) Pym's heroines try to please men and women who are part of the dominant culture, even though they may rebel inwardly against the dominant culture's bad taste or manners.[15] Thus their feelings of success or failure are conceptualized in predominantly 'male ways' even though they create an inner dialectic that challenges the stereotypes.[16] Her heroines consequently always fight their battles on an internalized landscape rather than on an external ground of confrontation. Occasionally, the heroine's perceptions or judgements redefine external reality, as when Mildred puts off Everard Bone's invitation to cook his meat, Julian's proposal and Winifred's need for a refuge. These events are the real triumphs for Mildred in the novel.

Identifying three of Mildred's triumphs here suggests how negative and indefinite her language is in the novel. If success is equated with resistance and triumph with indefinite compromise or postponement, then the language that clothes these events is likely to be similarly constituted.

Even a glance at the language of the first ten pages of *Excellent Women* confirms this larger impression. In fact, Mildred's first words are rather defensive and negatively framed: when challenged by the pomposity of Mr Mallett, one of the churchwardens who remarks upon Mildred's knowledge of new neighbours moving in, she replies, 'Well, yes, one usually does [know about it] . . . It is rather difficult not to know such things' (*EW*, 5).[17] The indirection created by 'rather difficult not' distances Mildred and elevates the whole activity that Mr Mallett has implicated her in. When describing the arrangement of her apartment, she says, 'There were offices on the ground floor and above them the two flats, not properly self-contained and without every convenience' (*EW*, 6). One comes upon the negatives without warning and feels the prick of deflation.

These two linguistic patterns do not simply point out an ironic discrepancy. They act doubly: first, they distance Pym's heroine from the impression as it might be expressed by a member of the dominant class; then they also suggest a doubleness within the heroine. She is not only a subordinate (i.e. different from Mr Mallett or from someone who would live in a flat properly self-contained and with every convenience); she is also compensated for this difference by a humourous enjoyment of it, tied up as that difference is with the qualities she most likes about herself (her independence, for instance, in having her own flat).[18]

In those novels by Pym where I have found these linguistic patterns but where Pym has not used a first person narration, the irony works very similarly. Though the narration is in the third person, the ironic subversion of convention generally occurs in cases where the narrator and heroine are indistinguishable. Belinda in *Some Tame Gazelle* sounds very much like Mildred in *Excellent Women* when she is thinking about how to prevent the new curate from allowing his long underwear to show: 'Of course he might think it none of their business, as indeed it was not, but Belinda rather doubted whether he thought at all, if one were to judge by the quality of his first sermon' (*STG*, 7). Also like the subversive irony in *Excellent Women*, the ironic viewpoint of these heroines is often turned on themselves. They are often painfully aware of their own shortcomings, as when Belinda confesses, ' "I don't sweep rooms, Emily does that. The things I do seem rather useless, but I suppose it [a quotation mentioned earlier] could be applied to any action of everyday life, really" ' (*STG*, 68). But the humility of the heroine is what empowers her in Pym's novel; it supports her judgements. That last remark of Belinda's is followed by a sharp judgement of Donne's patronizing manner: ' "Oh certainly, Miss Bede", said Mr Donne, with curately heartiness. "We cannot all have the same gifts", he added, with what Belinda felt was an insufferably patronizing air' (STG, 68). The inversion of her humility into a distanced judgement in no way belies the humility. They have a complementary relation. Also, Belinda resents having her self-deprecatory comment put in a competitive context as the curate does. Its self-examining purpose is thus demeaned. (The codes that characterize the inner lives of Pym's male characters tend to be self-complacency and social competition.)

With the less aware female characters in her novels, Pym's irony is no less severe than with her male characters. For instance, in *Jane and Prudence*, the narrator describes Prudence and Fabian at a dinner which is supposedly very romantic but where both have hearty appetites: 'Prudence chose what she would have, perhaps more carefully than a woman truly in love would have done' (JP, 102). Fabian is the butt of keener irony than Prudence, but female characters like Prudence, Barbara Bird in *Crampton Hodnet*, Deirdre in *Less than Angels*, or Harriet in *Some Tame Gazelle*, are subject to the narrator's irony because they are either genuinely young and stupid or they pretend to youth and cultivate its stupidities. (Prudence and Harriet are guilty of the latter.) In either case these female characters lack or ignore the consciousness of their subordinate state necessary to transform subordination into an acutely-felt sensibility. This sensibility is reserved for a few female characters (ones I have called 'heroines'), the narrators and the readers of Pym's novels.

These heroines act like narrators in the way they keep their distance from the silliness of the other characters in the novels, and they are all observers more than actors, often drawn into the action somewhat against their wills. Their isolation, not their lack of intelligence or identity, relegates them to subordinate status, but their private views are intriguingly brought forward by Pym.[19] Though they may be subordinates in relation to a dominant culture's assumptions, the reader and the narrator join them in that isolation. That redefinition by the fictional universe, in turn, empowers their sensibility.

Interestingly, while Pym creates convincing friendships between female characters, as for example between Jane and
Prudence or Harriet and Belinda, these friendships do not
impinge on the heroine's isolation. The female characters in
these friendships have complementary rather than like personalities, allowing each some distance from the other, but not
inviting confidences between them. In the rare cases when Pym
inserts two heroines in a novel, as she does when she includes
both Jessie Morrow and Jane Cleveland in *Jane and Prudence*,
the two may take each other's measure, acknowledging each
other's acuity, but circumstances tend to limit each to her own
sphere. Jane and Jessie find themselves separated by Fabian's
fickleness. Jane assesses Jessie's strategy when she discovers
Jessie's triumph:

> Perhaps this was after all what men liked to come home to,
> someone restful and neutral, who had no thought of changing the
> curtains or wallpapers? Jessie, who, for all her dim appearance,
> was very shrewd, had no doubt realised this. A beautiful wife
> would have been too much for Fabian, for one handsome person is
> enough in a marriage, if there is to be any beauty at all. (*JP*, 193)

Jessie's misunderstanding, Jane's, the reader's and the narrator's all coalesce here in a paradigmatic generalization that
indirectly sums up Fabian's (and, to some extent, all men's)
character.

The subversiveness of the heroines and of the narrators
allows them to challenge the complacency of the male and
female characters around them who conform to the dominant
culture. But these challenges promote private laughter and a
critical examination of their own assumptions too. They take
place in an inner private space shared by narrator, heroine and
reader rather than in the public space of the interaction
between characters.[20]

Notes

1. [*Editor's note:* The thicker slice of bread is evidence of Helena's lack of

refinement and slapdash methods of housekeeping as well. Mildred's idea of a gracious tea includes her 'best coffee cups and biscuits on little silver dishes', while Helena is proud of serving tea in mugs (*EW*, 6).] Mildred's eager taking of the bread, then, ironically associates her with the woman she has just criticized even before she explicitly questions the conventional character of her criticism.

2. Jane Austen, *Pride and Prejudice* (New York: Washington Square Press, 1973), p. 1.
3. See the analysis of Austen's irony in these texts: Reuben Arthur Brower, *The Fields of Light: An Experiment in Critical Reading* (Oxford: Oxford University Press, 1951); Marvin Mudrick, *Jane Austen: Irony as Defense and Discovery* (Princeton: Princeton University Press, 1952); and Dorothy Van Ghent, 'On *Pride and Prejudice*' in *The English Novel: Form and Function* (New York: Holt, Rinehart, and Winston, 1953), pp. 99–111.
4. See Jane Nardin's comments on male characters in Pym's novels in *Barbara Pym* (Boston: Twayne, 1985), pp. 43–4, 89–91.
5. Both Hélène Cixous and Julia Kristeva suggest that women's language is not the exclusive province of female authors and that avant-garde male writers such as Joyce achieve some of the features (such as indefiniteness, openness and a concern for process) that have been claimed for a female style (as by Virginia Woolf). Pym's fiction is not without sympathetic male characters. [*Editor's note*: See Diana Benet's comments on Rupert in *An Unsuitable Attachment* in her *Something to Love: Barbara Pym's Novels* (Columbia: University of Missouri Press, 1986), p. 105.] But they are sympathetic only in a relative way within the ruthless imperfect world of comedy, and they are found in the later, darker Pym novels from which the bemused, modest, narrator-like heroines I am examining are missing.
6. Jean Baker Miller, *Toward a New Psychology of Women* (Boston: Beacon Press, 1976), pp. 6–12.
7. Miller, p. 6.
8. *Ibid.*, p. 7.
9. See *ibid.*
10. See *ibid.*, p. 10.
11. See *ibid.*, p. 49.
12. See *ibid.*, pp. 52–3.
13. See *ibid.*, pp. 54–6.
14. See *ibid.*, pp. 71–3.
15. See *ibid.*, pp. 56–9.
16. The sense of success or failure in interaction has been explored by Pamela M. Fishman, 'What Do Couples Talk about When They're Alone?' in Douglas Butturff and Edmund L. Epstein (eds), *Women's Language and Style* (Akron: University of Akron, 1978), pp. 11–22.
17. See Muriel R. Schulz's comments on vague qualifiers, hedges, and dodges in Virginia Woolf's fiction, in 'A Style of One's Own', *Women's Language and Style*, p. 76; and Robin T. Lakoff's cautious comments

on defensive strategies, in 'Women's Language', *Women's Language and Style*, p. 155.

18. See Lakoff on Politeness, *Women's Language and Style*, p. 157, and in her 'Language and Woman's Place', *Language in Society*, 2 (1973): 56.

19. An explanation of what they call 'the female register', or the way speech reflects subordinate status, is found in Faye Crosby and Linda Nyquist, 'The Female Register: An Empirical Study of Lakoff's Hypotheses', *Language in Society*, 6 (1977): 313–22; in Mary Ritchie Key, *Male/Female Language* (Methuchen, NJ: Scarecrow Press, 1975); and in Barrie Thorne and Nancy Henley (eds), *Sex and Language* (Rowley, Mass.: Newbury House, 1975).

20. Consider Nelly Furman's analysis of Virginia Woolf's spatial metaphors in '*A Room of One's Own:* Reading Absence', *Women's Language and Style*, pp. 99–105.

Chapter 6

Glamourous Acolytes: Homosexuality in Pym's World

CHARLES BURKHART

Homosexuality in fiction is a difficult subject, especially with a writer like Barbara Pym, who is more conventional than revolutionary. Superficially it is an unlikely ingredient of the Anglican tea parties and jumble sales or of the bureaucracy and suburbia she writes about. Some of the difficulties in any consideration of the subject are, first, that some writers, themselves not homosexuals, write about homosexuality, as Norman Mailer has done in *Ancient Evenings*. Some, themselves homosexuals, write about the subject, like Proust, but their aim is a general audience. Still other writers are homosexual and write about homosexuality, and seem to aim at the homosexual reader: perhaps Firbank fulfils all three of these particular terms. Further, the categories tend to merge, because who knows what homosexuality is? Is it merely statistical? Is its source cultural or genetic? Is it sometimes only a fad which a contemporary novelist feels obliged to acknowledge? And can it even be called, as it often now is, a central factor, though one which is usually mislabelled, in the androgynous ideal? To illustrate the central role homosexuality plays in Barbara Pym's novels is less to define it than to reveal her large-scaled impartial tolerance, and this intrinsic morality is one of the best reasons we have for liking and admiring her books. Our notion that she is a conventional writer evanesces, to be replaced by the recognition that her range is bolder than we might have thought.

Whatever homosexuality is, it is widely there, and it appears in all twelve novels by Barbara Pym which have so far been published. Of the novelists just mentioned she herself, though certainly not homosexual by any ordinary definition, is most like Firbank. In fact one of her very early novels, *Young Men in Fancy Dress*, is clearly influenced by him. It also echoes, as does her later fiction, two other writers of debatable sexuality, Evelyn Waugh and Ivy Compton-Burnett. One of the appeals of these three writers to Barbara Pym, herself a comic novelist, is their comedy. Their comic sensibility suited hers, and like any other artist, she made use of whatever suited her to help evolve her own unique way of looking at the world. Her attraction to these writers seems almost chemical; as mysterious as chemistry, her interest in Firbank and Waugh and Compton-Burnett precipitated a variety of awakenings and accomplishments in her creative laboratory. What apparently did not attract her was other elements in them, like Waugh's sourness or Firbank's stillness or Compton-Burnett's powerful, grim coldness. Pym was more equable, more harmonious, more serene. Although she knew, in Catherine Oliphant's words, that life was 'comic and sad and indefinite', her novels with all their hilarity end in a sort of serenity, or acceptance, or even optimism (*LTA*, 89).

I think it was the gaiety of gay people that she liked. If this and some of my other remarks on gay people seem stereotypical, my defence must be that there is always some truth behind stereotypes, no matter how negative and deplorable we would prefer to find them; and that Barbara Pym shared them. The most acute of observers, she found some generalizations about gay people congenial, and there is little evidence that she questioned the generalizations or dwelt upon exceptions to them. A novelist tends to make character representative, not just as a fictional shorthand but as a sop to our urge for order. Nor were her observations less shrewd for that concession. One of the pleasures of fiction is that it codifies experience for us. The diversity might otherwise dishearten or appal. There are large autobiographical elements submerged in Barbara Pym's portrayals of homosexuals, and thus her generalizations may have served some saving purpose of their own. Perhaps the life of Barbara Pym that Hazel Holt is writing may particularize some of these relations between her life and her books. Once in a while characters appear like Coco in *An Academic Question* who are obviously closely modelled on someone she knew.

But most of her gay men are presented with the same objectivity that distinguishes her other characters. It is interesting that she wrote nothing on overt lesbian attachments. There are female pairings or bondings from the first novel published in her lifetime (*Some Tame Gazelle*, 1950) to the last she wrote (*A Few Green Leaves*, published posthumously in 1980). They are always funny. Edith Liversidge in *Some Tame Gazelle*, who wears a 'mannish navy blue overcoat', has befriended Connie Aspinall, a 'decayed gentlewoman' in trailing garments who 'plays the harp very beautifully' (*STG*, 183, 15). Edith bosses Connie, calling her like a dog when she wants her, and invites the heroine Belinda to a supper with them of bread and tinned baked beans, into which she absentmindedly drops 'a grey wedge of ash' (*STG*, 184). In *A Few Green Leaves*, Miss Lee is the more active type, her friend Miss Grundy the more passive. In *Excellent Women* the flat on the floor below that of the heroine, Mildred Lathbury, is rented, after the departure of the Napiers, by a couple whose appearance is marked by a sly use of symbols:

> I walked quietly up the stairs, not wanting to meet them yet, but I was just passing what I shall always think of as the Napiers' kitchen when a sharp but cultured woman's voice called out, 'Is that Miss Lathbury?'
>
> I stood transfixed on the stairs and before I had time to answer a small grey-haired woman, holding a tea-caddy in her hand, put her head out of the door.
>
> 'I'm Charlotte Boniface', she announced. 'My friend Mabel Edgar and I are just moving in—as you can see.' She gave a little laugh.
>
> Another pair of women, I thought with resignation, feeling a little depressed that my prophecy had come true, but telling myself that after all they were the easiest kind of people to have in the house.
>
> 'Edgar!' called Miss Boniface into the other room. 'Come and meet Miss Lathbury, who lives in the flat above us.'
>
> A tall grey-haired woman holding a hammer in her hand came out and smiled in a mild shy sort of way. (*EW*, 242)

In another novel of the 1950s, the most interesting duo of all appears: the bluff and snorting librarian, Esther Clovis, who has 'hair like a dog', and her equally assertive friend Gertrude

Lydgate, who pursues linguistic oddities among the tribes of Africa, including pygmies. All such female pairs in the novels are only observations, not comments.

There are ten times more male homosexuals, and they are more pointedly presented, especially in Pym's early and rather amateur novel *Crampton Hodnet*, which was not resurrected for publication until 1985, five years after her death. It is an Oxford novel where among the 'conceited and effeminate' undergraduates two students with saintlike names, Michael and Gabriel, are conspicuous (*CH*, 68). They are skittish and voluble, speak in italics, call each other 'my dear' and practise ballet steps in the Botanical Gardens. If they seem the creations of a very young author, which they are, they reappear in the person of Terry Skate in the late novel *A Few Green Leaves*, a character who, when he meets the rector Tom Dagnall, is described as 'a young man with golden bobbed hair, dressed in the usual T-shirts and jeans and wearing pink rubber gloves, an unusual and slightly disturbing note' (*FGL*, 63). But Terry is integrated into the story in a way that those butterflies Michael and Gabriel in *Crampton Hodnet* are not. Terry is a florist who decorates the mausoleum of Tom's church, and that is about as far as his faith goes. He eventually loses it and abandons the job because 'those talks on the telly' about religion have alienated him (*FGL*, 199). He promises Tom that he and his 'friend' would ' "be happy to assist you if you were having another flower festival or anything like that. . . . And we do weddings, as you know. Cheerio then, rector" ' (*FGL*, 200). Blithely exiting, he leaves Tom to his flowerless mausoleum; Tom is an inadequate shepherd whose sheep have gone astray.

In another later novel, *An Academic Question*, the character Coco drifts as pointlessly in and out of the text as do Michael and Gabriel. Like them, unlike Terry, he has no easy thematic value; he was only someone Barbara Pym knew and was fascinated by. She was too close to him to make him more than an element of the texture of this arbitrary story. Perhaps, as the confidante of the heroine Caro, he serves as a more sympathetic ear than does her husband, the boorish Alan, who suggests ironically that Coco is ' "[like a] sister" ' to her (*AQ*, 12). Occupying an unlikely position at the provincial univer-

sity where the novel takes place, something to do with research
on Caribbean immigrants, Coco is concerned with two
subjects—clothes and his mother—a fact that may make its
own stereotypical comment. Perhaps he serves to illustrate
Caro's paucity of options for relationships. At least he is
responsible for one intelligent exchange between Caro and the
predatory lecturer Iris, who asks Caro if Coco is homosexual:
' "We've never talked about it" ', Caro answers. She goes on
to make a pointed distinction: ' "In any case, are people to be
classified as simply that? Some people just love themselves" '
(AQ, 65).

These extreme examples of camp sensibility—Michael,
Gabriel, Terry and Coco—are noticeable, even striking, but
there are other men, and they are much more usual than this
flashy group of four, who are not one thing or another. In
Something to Love: Barbara Pym's Novels, Diana Benet
comments on men who 'do not seem very interested in, or
curious about, the opposite sex as a whole'.[1] It is likely that
they are destined for celibacy. In *Excellent Women* we find
both William Caldicote, a 'fussy' gourmet, who occasionally
has lunch with Mildred Lathbury, and a friend of his from
Oxford days whom Mildred had known, 'a willowy young
man of a type that does not look as if it would marry' (*EW*,
122).

Gourmets like William are quite common in Barbara Pym's
books. One does not exactly like to rush to the conclusion that
sex and food are the same thing, but there are intimations that
this is so. William is vigorously opposed to the institution of
marriage; referring to the Napiers, he deplores ' "all these
delightful men married to such monsters, such fiends" ' (*EW*,
69). He may not be an authority on marriage, but he is
particular indeed about wine properly 'chambré'. Adam
Prince, in *A Few Green Leaves*, is a gourmet by profession, as
his 'soft, plump body' shows, and he evaluates restaurants for
a living; he is constantly obsessed by questions such as *had* the
celery 'come out of a tin?' and was the mayonnaise '*really*
home-made?' (*FGL*, 25). These men are not without their
problems; William's office has been moved, and now different
pigeons come to his window to be fed; Adam, though he looks
'the very picture of health, fat and sleek as a well-living

neutered cat', tells old Dr Gellibrand that he is suffering, he believes, from 'tension or stress—isn't that the fashionable word?' (*FGL*, 207).

Wilfrid Bason, in *A Glass of Blessings*, is the most out-rageous of the food fanciers and one of Barbara Pym's most comic characters. His genial dizziness makes him one of the best of the pushy and precious. As cook to the clergy house, he brings splendid or at least artful cuisine to the clergy: ' "Do you know" ', confides Father Thames to Wilmet, ' "he has promised us a *coq au vin*?" ' (*GB*, 60). There is a lot to be said against Wilf: he is gushy, with his 'rather fluty enthusiastic voice', he listens at doors, and he is even a thief, purloining a Fabergé egg from the collection of his employer (*GB*, 55). It would have to have been an egg, since he has an egg-shaped head; and he later acquires an egg-shaped beard: 'I thought my face just needed something, and a beard did seem to provide the finishing touch, as it were' (*GB*, 245). In his delightful and deplorable way he is the liaison between the world of the church and Piers's world, the ambiance of the homosexual protagonist; he is a friend of young Keith, who is Piers's lover.

Barbara Pym knew a lot about food, and she knew a great deal about the church. It is interesting that Adam Prince 'had once been a Church of England clergyman before his doubting of the validity of Anglican Orders had sent him over to Rome' (*FGL*, 26). Wilf says that 'Celibacy of the clergy has always been *our* motto', but one wonders if it is his own (*GB*, 237). Are there homosexual clergymen in Barbara Pym's novels? In *The Pleasure of Miss Pym* I wrote that 'One is happy to report, for the sake of that institution, that in Barbara Pym's church there are no homosexual clergymen'.[2] But this now strikes me as a hasty generalization. There are in-between types, like the handsome and unmarried Father Neville Forbes in *No Fond Return of Love*, or in *An Unsuitable Attachment* the 'tame' (as he is twice called) Father Basil Branche, whose cigarette holder is 'rather too long' (*UA*, 165). Sophia, one of the heroines of that novel, says of him, ' "I'm sure Father Branche *is* rather delicate, you know. He doesn't look at all strong and it would be a great strain trying to be manly all the time" ' (*UA*, 170). Too devout a churchwoman ever to dwell on their possible departures from chastity, Barbara Pym none the less includes a curate among the lovers of Colin, a minor character in *The Sweet Dove Died*, and one of the 'glamourous acolytes' (the phrase appears in *Excellent Women*, 33) in *A Glass of Blessings* is heard to say in 'a shrill mean voice', ' "Ooh, Bill, look how you've parked the car!" ' (*GB*, 100). The church is not immune from homosexuality, as Sybil Forsyth, the heroine's agnostic mother-in-law, rejoices in pointing out early in the book:

> 'Ah, yes, the *Church Times*,' said Sybil, 'with a few tempting titbits to encourage suitable applicants [for the position of assistant priest in the local church]. Vestments—Western Use—large robed choir—opportunities for youth work. Though perhaps *not* the last—we know the kind of thing that sometimes happens: the lurid headlines in the gutter press or the small sad paragraph in the better papers.' (*GB*, 15)

Nor will she drop the subject when on the following day she unintentionally misreads book titles at a shop she is visiting with Wilmet: ' "*Victory over Pan*," she read, and "*My Tears at the Vatican*. I wonder what *that* can be? The autobiography of some poor unfortunate priest of the type we were talking about last night?" ' (*GB*, 23). Sybil's insistence prepares us for the gradual revelation that Piers Longridge himself, in whom Wilmet conceives a romantic interest, though not a clergyman, is gay. The church is not pictured as a hotbed of or refuge for homosexuality, but Barbara Pym knew that it was there.

Still a third area in which she was personally experienced is the academic world of libraries, research institutes and universities. Mervyn Cantrell in *An Unsuitable Attachment* may want to marry Ianthe Broome, his librarian assistant, for her Pembroke table and Hepplewhite chairs, but his sexual tastes lie elsewhere. Ianthe visits Mervyn's former employee, a crusty pensioner named Miss Grimes:

> 'Now tell me the library gossip', said Miss Grimes. 'What's this new young man like? More to our Mervyn's taste than a girl, I shouldn't wonder.' She gave Ianthe a sly look.
>
> Really, she wasn't a very nice old woman, thought Ianthe, beginning to feel indignant. (*UA*, 77)

Edward Killigrew, a Bodleian librarian in *Crampton Hodnet*, has 'a fussy, petulant voice', takes pleasure in 'spiteful bits of gossip', and lives with his mother, a demanding old lady proud of her nearly eighty years (*CH*, 50). In *Less than Angels*, Mark Penfold, one of the students of that suave, rich old gentleman and retired anthropology professor, Felix Byron Mainwaring, says of both Felix and a fellow student, Tom Mallow, 'I don't imagine that Felix had such trouble with his girl friends—if they were that—as Tom is having now' (*LTA*, 187). In *Jane and Prudence*, the two heroines are talking about the Oxford career of Flora, Jane's daughter, and Flora's tutor at Oxford, who has the fine Donizettian name of Lord Edgar Ravenswood:

'. . . I'd hoped that Lord Edgar might fall in love with her—when they were at tutorials, you know.'
   'But he hates women, surely?' Prudence asked.
   'I know, that's the point. I'd imagined Flora breaking through all that.'
   Prudence laughed. (*JP*, 161)

Lord Edgar, Professor Mainwaring and Mervyn Cantrell are minor figures in the carpet. There are two homosexuals in the novels, however, who deserve comment in themselves because they are major figures in major novels, and because one is likeable, Piers Longridge in *A Glass of Blessings*, and the other is probably the least attractive character Pym created, Ned in *The Sweet Dove Died*. Somehow they represent learning experiences for Barbara Pym herself, but experiences which, unlike Coco for example, she has assimilated. Whatever the autobiographical impulse behind them, she is in full control of their believable functions in the two novels. One can only wonder at how the pain their prototypes—or prototype—must personally have engendered has undergone its saving transformation. Not to be too Freudian about it, Piers and Ned are dissonances in experience, which she beautifully resolved in her writing.
   Not that Piers is heroic. His appeal is that he is not. He drifts through odd jobs, like teaching and translating Portuguese; he collects numbers on automobile licence tags; he drinks too

much. He is mentioned in the first line in the novel and soon comes to dominate the imagination of the heroine, Wilmet Forsyth. Despite his diffident charm and rather lost quality, despite her romantic walks and luncheons with him, despite the contrast he offers to her monotonous bureaucratic husband and to a beefy old boyfriend who would like to become her lover, Wilmet might earlier have been warned by his response to her, as when she exuberantly admires some flowers in a park: ' "My dear, it isn't quite you, this enthusiasm", said Piers. "You must be cool and dignified, and behave perfectly in character—not plunging in among lupins" ' (GB, 189). He treats her like a beautiful immovable object. A Glass of Blessings is the story of Wilmet's education. When she at last discovers that Piers lives with his lover Keith, she weathers the shock with admirable restraint, though Piers is drawn to comment, ' "My dear girl, what's the matter? Do you think I've been deceiving you, or something absurd like that?" ' (GB, 198). Both a good deal younger and of lower social background than Piers, Keith poses for illustrations of knitting patterns in catalogues and works evenings in a coffee bar called La Cenerentola. He is quite interested in detergents and curtain linings; governessy with Piers; altogether admiring of the elegant Wilmet, who in turn begins to find him not only remarkably good looking but, ruefully, rather a dear. And so Wilmet returns to her own life—her dull husband, her excellent church work, most of all to her wit and grace. Piers disappears. Wilmet's foray into his world has done her no lasting damage, instead it may have enriched her with the one quality her glass of blessings lacked, that which George Herbert in his poem called 'rest'. She was one of Barbara Pym's favourite heroines.

Another elegant woman, Leonora Eyre, is the heroine of The Sweet Dove Died, written around twenty years later and one of Barbara Pym's best novels (the other two, I would say, are Less than Angels and Quartet in Autumn). There is more than a twenty years' contrast here. Leonora's opponent for the affections of James, decades her junior, is at first Phoebe, a young woman of his own age who loses, and then Ned, a young man of his own age who wins. But Ned returns to his native America and other conquests, leaving James, who has never made up his mind about anything, and the defeated Leonora behind—to her exquisite taste, her Victorian bibe- lots, her elderly admirers, her sexual frigidity and her con- sciousness of death, viewed in terms consistent with this aim: 'there was no reason why one's death should not, in its own way, be as elegant as one's life, and one would do everything possible to make it so' (*SDD*, 18). She is a terrifying study of the enervations, even the ravages, of taste; it is all she has, and it virtually destroys her. Though she and Wilmet are alike in some ways, the contrast between gentle Wilmet's ironic realizations and Leonora's obsession with her style and her defeat show the remarkable detachment and control that Barbara Pym had achieved in her writing.

Leonora's opponent Ned is as formidable as Keith (that banal and beautiful boy) was not. There is nothing to be said to redeem him; his Guerlain and his interest in Keats are only weapons against her; he is predatory, poisonous, fickle, capri- cious, malicious and false, and he has a nasal American voice like a bee. He and Leonora are most suitable combatants in that they are both monsters of egotism; but he is ruthless, and she is fading and frail beside him. Ned exemplifies the direr side of human behaviour, not just homosexual behaviour; but it is clear that his promiscuity and general bitchiness are an embodiment of hostile homosexual clichés.

The other major novel of Barbara Pym's late career is *Quartet in Autumn*. It has the fewest references to homo- sexuality of any of her novels; at the same time it is the most naturalistic of them, the most acute and relentless in its depiction of people. Despite its authoritative analysis of illness and senility, of bureaucracy, the welfare state and in fact modern Britain itself, it is her most objective work. Whatever role homosexuality had played in her life it is now not so much confronted as finally effaced. In her last years she had come to terms, and how triumphantly she had done so is shown by the comedy of *Quartet*, glittering, surrealistic and brisk.

Throughout the twelve novels, straight men are most of the time rather terrible creatures. She once protested that she '*loved*' men, but her novels do not show that she did. How often are her men preposterously vain, selfish, self-pitying and self-indulgent: men who use women, women who too often acquiesce because they have to. Anyone who has read Barbara Pym's work has noticed it. From the asperities of Archdeacon Hoccleve in *Some Tame Gazelle* to the flabby vanities of Graham Pettifer in *A Few Green Leaves*, straight men are out for what they can get, and the way the world is, they usually succeed. In a sense the homosexual men, or some of them, are a solace, though by no means a solution. For every pale and ineffectual curate there is a Wilf Bason; she had met him and knew him, and her experience and knowledge can enlarge and instruct our own. Her world is not so narrow after all.

Notes

1. Diana Benet, *Something to Love: Barbara Pym's Novels* (Columbus: University of Missouri Press, 1986), p. 59.
2. Charles Burkhart, *The Pleasure of Miss Pym* (Austin: University of Texas Press, 1987), p. 93.

PART THREE: LITERARY HERITAGE

Pym's extensive use of literary allusion in her fiction is remarkable for its breadth and variety. While up at Oxford University, she joked with friends about 'The Bond of Our Greater English Poets', and she continued to quote freely from their works in her own writing through the years. Yet her ingenious use of English literature extends beyond snatches of quotation from poetry to substantial reworking of earlier novels. The following essays offer extended studies of covert or hidden allusions in Pym's fiction, in particular her reworking of several elements of Austen's *Emma* in *A Glass of Blessings*, and her rewriting of Brontë's *Jane Eyre* in various pieces throughout her literary career. These major nineteenth-century novels seem to have exercised considerable influence on Pym's writing, and they contribute to the sense of anachronism in her contemporary yet deliberately old-fashioned fiction. Pym clearly conceived of her writing within the context of the rich tradition of the English novel, and her own 'modern' versions of old stories show her indebtedness to past heritage as well as her creativity in altering and shaping it further.

Chapter 7

A Glass of Blessings, Jane Austen's Emma, and Barbara Pym's Art of Allusion

JAN FERGUS

Barbara Pym's characters are notoriously allusive. The Archdeacon Henry Hoccleve's celebrated Judgment Day sermon in *Some Tame Gazelle,* which stupefies most of his congregation, merely exaggerates the passion for quoting from 'our greater English poets' shared by many of the characters in that novel (*STG*, 130).[1] Although in later novels most of Pym's major characters manage to restrain this passion somewhat, they still display extensive familiarity with the great tradition of English poetry and prose. Their allusions to poems, novels, Anglican hymns, and other literary works, are either 'overt' or 'covert'. An allusion is overt or explicit when characters or narrators openly mention authors or titles, or cite lines, characters, themes, or situations from works of literature. By contrast, a covert or implicit allusion occurs when the text provides no clear indication that allusion is present.

In Pym's novels, allusions are usually overt. When Wilmet Forsyth concludes that her life may have been 'a glass of blessings', she makes an overt and easily identified allusion to the poem by George Herbert that provides the novel with its title and epigraph (*GB*, 256). Similarly, when Piers Longridge says to Wilmet that 'We'll build in sonnets pretty rooms', he is alluding overtly to John Donne's poem 'The Canonization' (*GB*, 73). The allusion is overt even though neither the poet nor the title is mentioned. Despite Wilmet's possible failure to recognize the line, she does call attention to it when she comments that Piers speaks 'strangely' (*GB*, 73). In such cases, readers must draw upon their own knowledge of literature to identify the allusion, but if they fail to do so they will none the less usually find some humour or poignancy in the words themselves, taken in context.

An allusion is covert or implicit when no explicit reference is made to an author, title, line, character, theme or situation. As a result, the reader's own familiarity with literature is tested by covert allusions even more strenuously than by overt ones. Not just knowledge but tact is required, for the temptation to detect implicit allusions everywhere in Pym's works can be quite acute and must be resisted. Such allusions are thus difficult to exemplify unambiguously. When the narrator of *The Sweet Dove Died* tells us that 'It is a truth now universally acknowledged that owners grow to look like their pets', the allusion to the opening line of Jane Austen's *Pride and Prejudice* is covert because nothing indicates that quotation is occurring (*SDD*, 65).[2] The line is so familiar, however, that the allusion—though technically covert—is actually obvious and hilarious to most readers. They are likely to relish this comic conjunction between the marital relation (ironically viewed by Austen) and the relation to pets (a favourite Pym theme).

Most of Pym's novels after *Some Tame Gazelle* and *Excellent Women* allude overtly to Austen's works.[3] Perhaps *Less than Angels* and *No Fond Return of Love* include the most explicit references, citing *Persuasion* and *Mansfield Park* respectively (*LTA*, 186; *NFR*, 253). Although *A Glass of Blessings* includes no overt allusions to Austen's novels whatsoever, its covert references to *Emma* partially control both form and content so extensively that Pym can almost be said to have rewritten that novel. The handsome, clever, rich and snobbish heroines, Emma Woodhouse and Wilmet Forsyth, undergo severe humiliation for their errors in perceiving themselves and others. Revelation of their errors is eventually followed by some kind of moral regeneration. Less broad, more detailed parallels between the novels are also present; for example, between the ways Jane Fairfax and Mary Beamish operate as foils to the heroines. By combining such covert references to *Emma* with overt ones to other literature, Pym creates in *A Glass of Blessings* a highly sophisticated art of allusion, more

so than that in her earlier works.⁴ And finally she uses this art
to insist on an immense distance—both social and aesthetic—
between Austen's world and her own. Ultimately, then, Pym's
covert and overt allusions undercut the notion of a resemblance to Austen.

David Kubal in *The Hudson Review* first pointed out the
parallels between *Emma* and *A Glass of Blessings* in some
detail:

> Like Jane Austen's Emma, whom Miss Pym has in mind through-
> out the novel, Wilmet is not so much ill-used as unused; not so
> much tyrannized by her class, her bureaucratic husband, Rodney,
> and her mother-in-law, Sybil, as spoiled by them. . . . Piers
> Longridge is her Frank Churchill. . . . Finally, in a scene of high
> comedy and sharp pain, . . . he confronts her with his secret lover,
> Keith (his Jane Fairfax), a Pan-like male model, and accuses
> Wilmet of being incapable of affection. It is the first time anyone
> has told her anything near the truth, and in response she says to
> Mary Beamish (her Harriet Smith) 'sometimes you discover that
> you aren't as nice as you thought you were—that you're in fact
> rather a horrid person, and that's humiliating somehow.'⁵

In fact, the parallels between *Emma* and *A Glass of Blessings*
are more extensive than this account suggests, as well as
somewhat different. Although Kubal considers Mary Beamish
to be Wilmet's Harriet Smith, Mary operates instead as a Jane
Fairfax within the novel—a foil whose excellence makes the
heroine feel uneasy and spiteful, whose good qualities she
acknowledges only reluctantly. This reluctance helps to make
Wilmet blind to Mary's attractions and therefore surprised at
her marriage, rather in the way that Emma tends to underrate
Jane's attractiveness although she acknowledges her 'elegance'. Wilmet's response to Mary exposes her own faults, as
does Emma's response to Jane. Finally, both Mary Beamish's
and Jane Fairfax's marriages are brought about by the death of
an ailing, demanding and wealthy woman; Mrs Beamish takes
on Mrs Churchill's role. Neither Frank Churchill nor Mary
will any longer be tied to an invalid relative's bedside, but
more important, both can now support a spouse in comfort. In
thus making Marius depend on Mary Beamish to rescue him
from his uncomfortable room at the clergy house, Pym slightly

inverts Austen's subplot in which Frank rescues Jane.

Kubal is right that Piers does keep his relation to Keith hidden, as Frank Churchill does his to Jane, but Keith resembles Harriet Smith or even Mrs Elton far more than Jane Fairfax, particularly in his wonderfully vulgar description of his moving in with Piers or in his patronizing inspection of Wilmet's curtains (GB, 217, 219). Both novels, indeed, exploit the full comic possibilities of not only vulgarity but snobbery. Class distinctions are cherished with wonderful complacency by a number of characters in both works, but principally by the heroines. Emma is notoriously conscious of gradations between 'the second rate and third rate of Highbury', and very clear about their inferiority to herself (E, 155). Although Wilmet is somewhat less assured of her own superiority, she frequently registers distinctions of class—including Keith's common voice, Father Bode's low taste in food, Bason's presumption in wanting to join with her and Rodney in sending flowers to Mrs Beamish's funeral.

Wilmet's character, in fact, constitutes the most sustained and significant covert allusion to Austen's novel. Like Emma in many respects, Wilmet is finally like her in the most important: she is brought to recognize her faults of character. Perhaps a covert allusion to Emma is present in one of Pym's earliest formulations of ideas for A Glass of Blessings. She wrote in her Literary Notebook on 5 May 1955, 'The knowledge might come to me—and I dare say it would be a shock—that one wasn't a particularly nice person (selfish, unsociable, uncharitable, malicious even)' (VPE, 194). This sentence has some affinity with Austen's reported remark that in writing Emma, 'I am going to take a heroine whom no one but myself will much like'.[6] Austen's 'I' here refers to herself as author, however; the 'I' of Pym's formulation refers not to Pym herself but to the heroine who will eventually become Wilmet Forsyth. The self-protective alternation in this early formulation, between 'I' and the more detached 'one', is intensified by the time Wilmet utters her version of this perception to Mary Beamish. That is, Wilmet's version is couched in the even more detached second person: 'you're in fact rather a horrid person' (GB, 206). The attempt here to distance herself somewhat from a recognition of her faults even as she recognizes them resembles Emma's self-justifying reflections on her earliest error, her misinterpretation of Mr Elton's behaviour to Harriet Smith (*E*, 134–7). In any case, both heroines do eventually achieve some degree of regeneration, but it takes Wilmet longer to do so. Until the very end, she is frequently selfish, unsociable, uncharitable, malicious even—possibly more unlikeable on first reading than Austen's heroine.

Apparently Pym 'sometimes compared *A Glass of Blessings* [to *Emma*] when discussing her own work'.[7] According to Hazel Holt, these comparisons were quite broad: *Excellent Women*, like *Pride and Prejudice*, is the novel '*everyone* likes'; Pym 'felt about Wilmet rather as J[ane] A[usten] felt about Emma,' and *A Glass of Blessings* is, like *Emma*, more difficult than the earlier work, less easily appreciated.[8] Some of the difficulty in *A Glass of Blessings* arises because Wilmet is a less immediately appealing narrator than Mildred Lathbury, but a good deal arises from the darker tone and more complex texture of the novel. On the whole, the comedy is more chequered in *A Glass of Blessings*, the allusions more poignant—making the comic techniques more demanding, as in *Emma*.

An especially good example of the chequered, complex comedy created by overt and covert allusion occurs in an early chapter, when Wilmet donates blood and goes shopping with Mary Beamish. Throughout the novel, Wilmet's relation to Mary reveals her faults as clearly as Emma's relation to Jane Fairfax reveals her vanity and jealousy. In Chapter 6 Pym creates comic exchanges between Wilmet and Mary that remind us of Austen's in their insistence on rendering the amusing but none the less painful undercurrents that lie beneath the surface of polite conversation. Wilmet becomes the comic butt of an overt allusion, one that she herself makes to the parable of the wise virgins: Mary inspires Wilmet to contemplate the virgins' 'unpleasant character', presumably a reference to their unwillingness to share their prospects of heavenly reward (*GB*, 85). But the scene wittily reveals Wilmet's own unpleasantness, her selfishness and lack of generosity, not Mary's.

After Wilmet donates blood, following Mary's earlier

splendid and exasperating example, they shop for a dress for Mary, who irritates Wilmet into revealing depths of nastiness. Part of Wilmet's irritation arises from guilt. She constantly compares herself to Mary, just as Emma compares herself to Jane Fairfax, and in both heroines the comparison issues in a complex combination of jealousy, imitation and resentment. Wilmet is first made uncomfortable by the contrast between her own fashionable clothes and Mary's cheap ones. She then becomes snobbishly annoyed at 'taking all this trouble' over Mary, and her reflections acquire increasingly bitchy tones: 'what did it matter what she wore?' (GB, 80). When Mary reveals that the curate has asked her to call him Marius, Wilmet is further annoyed, deciding that 'she was making rather too much of the matter'—a judgement that, in the style of Austen's high comedy, applies more to Wilmet herself than to Mary.

Wilmet's annoyance leaves her particularly unwilling to respond to Mary's overtures toward closer friendship in the rest of the scene. Mary speaks of the sadness of the approach of winter; Wilmet counters with her acceptance of the 'comfortable aspects . . . fires and warm clothes' (GB, 83). Mary continues by quoting the first two lines of Walter de la Mare's poem 'Autumn'; Wilmet responds 'abruptly' and dismissively with ' "Yes, it's a good poem" ' (GB, 84). Mary has quoted the poem partly in order to express the poignancy of her own feelings, but in the context of Wilmet's exasperation the quotation becomes slightly comical. This complex combination of comedy and pathos is typical of Pym's allusive art. Such complexities generally arise when characters resort to literature in order to assert or understand themselves and in order to comprehend the significance of what happens in their lives. As a rule, to allude openly to literary works in Pym's novels is to search—comically, poignantly or ambiguously—for significant expression or for consolation. Typically, as it is here, the search is met with incomprehension or dismissal.

After quoting de la Mare, Mary looks at Wilmet 'intently', clearly expecting that Wilmet will disclose her own sadness. Although Wilmet remembers another line of the poem, she does not utter it, and her dislike of Mary reaches a snobbish climax:

I felt I could not bear to be invited to a womanly sharing of
confidences. I looked at her dispassionately and saw almost with
dislike her shining eager face, her friendship offered to me. What
was I doing sitting here with somebody who was so very much not
my kind of person? It was my own fault for getting involved with
St Luke's, I told myself unreasonably. (GB, 84)

These reflections then lead Wilmet to dismiss the subject by
'abruptly' declaring the poem to be a good one. When Mary
mentions reading much poetry, Wilmet announces that she
prefers novels and makes her escape: 'I could not bear to think
that she might have read my own favourite poems, and my one
idea now was to escape from her as quickly as I could' (GB,
84). Although Wilmet is capable of determining that Mary
irritates her because the 'contrast' to herself makes her 'feel
guilty and useless', this realization certainly does not prevent
her from dwelling on Mary's unpleasant goodness by contemplating the parable of the wise virgins (GB, 84–5). This
wonderful combination of perception and honesty with irritation and snobbery is what reminds us of Emma Woodhouse
and finally makes Wilmet a similarly appealing character.

Covert allusions to plot, characterization and social comedy
in *Emma* do not exhaust Pym's interest in obtaining effects
typical of that novel. Like Austen, for instance, she creates
telling ironies of character and structure. Amusingly, when
Rodney patronizes Harry as an ineffectual married flirt and
pities Rowena, he has already embarked on his flirtation with
Prudence Bates (GB, 138). Wilmet, who sometimes wishes to
patronize and improve Mary Beamish, ironically finds later
that she needs Mary's sponsorship to 'enter the charmed circle
of decorators' at the parish church (GB, 206). Earlier, Wilmet's anxious efforts to encourage Mr Bason to restore Father
Thames's Fabergé egg prove to be thoroughly unnecessary,
much like Emma's anxiety over breaking the news of Frank
Churchill's engagement to Harriet (GB, 183). Pym also follows Austen's thematic interest in exploring the relation between boredom and imagination. Both Wilmet and Emma rely
on their distorted and distorting imaginations to sustain them
in a world populated (in their view) largely by bores and
vulgarians. Wilmet's imagination, like Emma's, has some

affinity with the shoddy imaginative worlds created in popular fiction. When she is most in the grip of her infatuation with Piers, he perceives that she talks like 'one of the cheaper women's magazines' (GB, 190). Such an imagination helps to give Wilmet in her ordinary relationships something that she calls at first 'unsuitable detachment'—at that point ostensibly a detachment from the possibility that another woman might love her husband but really a detachment from Rodney himself (GB, 18).[9]

Various inversions to the main plot of Emma are more interesting, however, than such echoes and resemblances. Pym has written Emma without Mr Knightley, and consequently without the high, secure moral standards that he represents. A modern version of the novel must do without these. She retains Mr Knightley in his other role, however, as unlikely romantic hero. To imitate Austen's strategy in presenting the heroine with an unlikely lover, Pym makes him the heroine's husband of a decade. Like Mr Knightley, Rodney Forsyth is a man whose long, familial relation with the heroine makes her unwilling to see him as a potentially romantic figure. After misreading Piers much as Emma in her vanity misreads Frank Churchill, and after ignoring the signs that Sybil will marry Professor Root, Wilmet learns that she has misread Rodney equally. He is still capable of romantic attachment and has in fact been seeing another woman. Indications of his interest in Prudence Bates are present but concealed, rather like the hints in Emma of Jane's and Frank's relationship before Mr Knightley suspects it. (These hints may be somewhat less obscure to readers who know Prudence's character from Jane and Prudence.) Indications that Piers is homosexual have been almost as obvious as the signs that Mr Elton is courting Emma herself, not Harriet Smith. As Charles Burkhart has observed, Wilmet 'seems to be the only person in the novel who does not know that . . . Piers Longridge . . . is homosexual'.[10] Wilmet remains resolutely blind to all clues about Rodney's and Piers's sexuality. Only when Sybil on her marriage to Professor Root ejects her son and his wife from her house—an extremely radical inversion of Mr Woodhouse's behaviour—are Wilmet and Rodney forced to become close enough to revaluate their relationship.

Once Rodney confesses his dinners with Prudence, and Wilmet her lunches with Piers and Harry, both dissolve into 'helpless laughter'—Pym's substitute for the kind of knowledge and intimacy that Emma and Mr Knightley achieve at the end of *Emma* (*GB*, 250). Their intimacy is not really qualified by Emma's failure to disclose to Mr Knightley Harriet's infatuation with him, although Austen's narrator may seem to qualify it in the often-quoted statement that 'Seldom, very seldom, does complete truth belong to any human disclosure' (*E*, 431). Although Wilmet asserts that 'now all is revealed', neither she nor Rodney actually reveals much (*GB*, 250). *Emma* without Mr Knightley cannot end with openness, certainty and security, as Austen's novel does.

This treatment of Wilmet and Rodney's marriage puts Pym at a great distance socially and aesthetically from Austen's world. And distance is evident also in the original conception of the novel. Nothing in the surviving manuscript version of the first three chapters, entitled 'The Lime Tree Bower', bears out the notion that a relationship to Austen's novel was originally planned (MS PYM 17). For example, characters in 'Lime Tree Bower' resemble those in Austen's novel less than they do in the final version. Mrs Beamish is less selfish and tyrannical in the manuscript, also less wealthy.[11] She may have been made more like Austen's Mrs Churchill in the final version either because Pym was alluding to Austen's novel or because she was engaged in her usual process of revision— going over the characters to 'make them worse'.[12] But in fact, most of the characters are 'worse' in the manuscript. Rodney is less sympathetic there: 'The fundamental coldness of his nature and his total failure to understand her particular kind of jokes did not become apparent for some years' (MS PYM 17, f. 15). Similarly, Mary Beamish is less attractive in 'The Lime Tree Bower' than in the novel, more obnoxiously self-sacrificing.[13] In the manuscript, Wilmet's dislike of Mary seems more justifiable than it does in *A Glass of Blessings*. Indeed, the only major character who seems 'worse' in the novel than in 'The Lime Tree Bower' is Wilmet herself.

What the manuscript reveals, in fact, are major differences between the two novels. The church, not Austen's work, is central in Pym's original conception of *A Glass of Blessings*. At the same time, the manuscript reveals something of Pym's methods of construction. Her earliest notes seem quite far from the final version, as though she were encountering particular difficulty in formulating her novel. She wrote anxiously, 'WHAT IS MY NEXT NOVEL TO BE?' in an entry in her Literary Notebook for 15 May 1955, continuing with:

> It can begin with the shrilling of the telephone in Freddie Hood's church and end with the flame springing up—the new fire on Easter Saturday in the dark church. Hope and a blaze of golden forsythia round the font. But what about the middle? (*VPE*, 194)

The 'middle' is problematic, but in this formulation the church is clearly central. As Pym jots down tentative notes toward developing a 'middle', the church remains central. Allusions to *Emma* are wholly absent from this process of developing plot and character:

> Vicar of a fashionable or city church—very high—the kind of vicar who would be telephoned to luncheon, and I (?) hear the bell trilling in the middle of the service (lunchtime).
> I work in an office—have a friend who lives with her mother and is a church worker. I am attracted to her brother, who has lost his academic job through drink and scandal. He is a printer's reader for rare things (? what). The squalor of his flat. His friends? Called Torquil or Piers?
> An induction service somewhere?
> Could the scandal concern a curate? And his wife. The wife running away and he having to bear the burden. Or the curate wanting to marry would be bad enough. . . .
> Perhaps I am a widow and have a house with rather 'nice things'. (MS PYM 17, f. 1)[14]

The manuscript's only hint of Austen's fiction—though not specifically of *Emma*—is visible in Pym's tendency to organize her characters on the basis of carefully structured parallels and contrasts. On a page near the middle of the notebook containing the manuscript, she lines up her *dramatis personae*, generally conceived according to their contrasting attitudes to religion:

Characters

Wilmet Aubrey	Anglo Catholic
Rodney Aubrey (Noddy)	Solid Broad Church
Sybil Aubrey (his mother)	Agnostic

Rowena Staples (a friend of Wilmet's, married with children, living in the country with a flirty husband)

Mary Beamish—a splendid little woman on committees, blood donors etc. church worker at Noddy's church. Perhaps with an elderly mother, who dies and then she is liberated

Piers? brother of Rowena Longridge lapsed Anglo-Catholic and drunken proofreader. Connected with the Church of Fr Thames

Squirrel, his friend, who shares his flat. Crew-cut and wind-cheater. He is a model (little brown bear)

Keith

Raymond

Fr Norman Oswald Thames

Fr John Marius Ransom   in the Clergy house

Fr George Albert Bode

Mr Bason (Wilfred Bason) their housekeeper (MS PYM 17, f. 34)

Pym herself commented very self-consciously at the top of this page ' "Oh, I like a crowded canvas!", says BP', and this technique of organizing the crowd according to various parallels and contrasts brings her close to Austen even though the actual material does not. In the drafts of the first chapters, something is made of Piers's lapsed faith and of the religious opposition between Wilmet and Rodney, she High Church and he Low. Even Rowena's husband, originally called Aubrey, later 'old Harry Grinners', has a firm place within these churchy rankings in the first draft. When he objects to their vicar's High Church innovations, Wilmet 'remembered that

Aubrey was quite a power in the Church—people's Warden I believe' (MS PYM 17, f. 41).

In the final version of the novel, the church is central, but not as schematically as in 'The Lime Tree Bower'. Instead, its symbolic implications become significant in resolving the themes, particularly in Chapter 20. What the manuscript reveals is a great deal of initial fluidity in the conception of plot, character, even theme. When Pym adopts the persona of her central character in order to shape the story, she seems to obtain more freedom to experiment with various roles. The phrase on the first page of 'The Lime Tree Bower', 'Perhaps I am a widow', suggests a need for flexibility and openness in the initial stages of construction. The manuscript begins in the first person, but the second half of what is now the first chapter in *A Glass of Blessings* is cast in the third person, and the first person re-emerges before the end of the chapter.[15]

More interestingly, the manuscript reveals some of the complex ways in which allusions to other works of fiction contribute to the shaping of plot and character. In the final version, an exchange between Wilmet and Piers reveals that her unusual name is drawn from a heroine in a novel:

> 'But Wilmet, life is like that, you know. Like your name—so sad, and you so gay and poised.'
> I liked this description of myself and longed for him to say more.
> 'Did you know that my name came out of one of Charlotte M. Yonge's novels?' I asked him. 'My mother was very fond of them. But why do you think it sad?'
> 'Because it seems to be neither one thing nor the other', he said, rather mysteriously, and then fell silent. (*GB*, 72)

The manuscript clarifies the allusion: the novel is *The Pillars of the House*, serialized between 1870 and 1873 (MS PYM 17, f. 12). Its heroine, Wilmet Underwood, is beautiful like Wilmet Forsyth but, unlike her, an exemplary housekeeper and essential to her family. With her brother's help, she raises ten younger brothers and sisters, becoming hardened in the process and later softened by marriage. The allusion to Yonge's heroine might seem, then, to be ironic, pointing to Wilmet Forsyth's continual feeling of uselessness. But when the allusion first occurs in the manuscript of *A Glass of Blessings*, the heroine is not useless, or at least not jobless. She works with Piers at the press. Pym there exploits the name for its ambiguity; her heroine (with a different surname) notes that her Christian name was

> an advantage in some ways, for authors often wrote Wilmet Aubrey, Esq. when objecting to my queries on their works. How much more angry they would have been had they known it was *Mrs.* Wilmet Aubrey who . . . dared to . . . tamper with their footnotes or to doubt their quotations! (MS PYM 17, f. 12)

The final version of the novel incorporates this ambiguity in gender more subtly. Piers seems to detect it when he 'mysteriously' comments that Wilmet's name is 'sad . . . neither one thing nor the other' (*GB*, 72). His comment and his silence may hint at his own unconventional sexuality; if so, Wilmet as usual—comically and poignantly—misses the point, although the reader need not, even if he is unacquainted with Yonge's novel. An allusion that may seem to be more obscure in the final version (because the title of Yonge's novel is dropped) has actually become more open and accessible.[16]

In general, allusions are more accessible and less intrusive in *A Glass of Blessings* than in 'The Lime Tree Bower'. The elaborate but covert allusions to *Emma* that developed at some later stage of writing manage to be both accessible and obscure. They seem to serve very complex purposes. Although Pym has emphatically said, 'I have never consciously tried to imitate Jane Austen', she appears to have had *Emma* very much in mind in *A Glass of Blessings*.[17] If the allusions are, as I suspect, conscious, then an important question remains: why did Pym choose to present them covertly? I suggest that her reasons were twofold. First, Pym would be very wary of inviting comparison to Austen overtly. In a talk to the Romantic Novelists' Association on 8 March 1978, she remarked:

> people have often asked me what other writers have influenced me—whether I started off trying to write about Jane Austen-ish themes in a modern setting. Of course I had no thought of this at all—I have already said (in a radio talk) that nobody would really

dare to attempt such a thing, but I do admit to having been
influenced by Elizabeth (the author of Elizabeth and her German
Garden) and, later, Ivy Compton-Burnett. But I have always tried
to write in my own way. (MS PYM 98, f. 80)

Overt borrowing from Austen would be both presumptuous
('nobody would really dare') and humiliating ('I have always
tried to write in my own way').

Second, Pym is very aware that the world her characters
inhabit is not Austen's. The treatment of Rodney and Wilmet's
relationship offers only one example of distance from Austen.
Wilmet is less at home in her world than Emma or any Austen
heroine. The world of Pym's characters seems far smaller than
Austen's, much more fragmented and threatening. Her
heroines, despite jobs and higher education, often seem to
have fewer options than Austen's heroines do, and entering
larger or different worlds can be an even trickier business for
them than for Anne Elliot, who explores the various worlds of
Uppercross, Lyme and Bath, or even Fanny Price, at Mansfield
and Portsmouth.[18] Wilmet strikes a characteristically tentative and ambivalent note near the end of A Glass of Blessings
when she reflects:

> It was both exciting and frightening to think how many different
> worlds I knew—or perhaps 'had knowledge of' would be a more
> accurate way of putting it. I could not say that I really knew the
> worlds of Piers and Keith, or even of Mr Coleman and his Husky if
> it came to that. It seemed as if the Church should be the place
> where all worlds could meet, and looking around me I saw that in
> a sense this was so. If people remained outside it was our—even
> my—duty to try to bring them in. (GB, 209)

'Perhaps', 'should', 'could', 'in a sense', 'if'—these uncertain-
ties help to make the world of Pym's novels a more difficult
place than Austen's characters inhabit, and render her social
comedy less stable.

Differences between Austen's social world and Pym's are
most significantly reflected in the techniques that bring about
a resolution in Chapter 20 of A Glass of Blessings. Although
Wilmet has earlier undergone several humiliating experiences,

and has partially recognized her faults, her moral regeneration is delayed until she visits Mary at the retreat house in this chapter. After Piers has criticized her snobbery and her inability to love in Chapter 17, she has acknowledged to Mary that 'sometimes you discover that you aren't as nice as you thought you were—that you're in fact rather a horrid person, and that's humiliating somehow' (*GB*, 199, 205–6). As Nardin points out, Wilmet's humiliation 'reminds the reader of *Emma*'.[19] But unlike Emma, she does not achieve regeneration as an immediate consequence of humiliation. Before she enters the retreat house, she is either 'belittling' herself, as Mary says, or congratulating herself on being able to 'inspire love in others' (Harry), or becoming dismayed at the prospect of sharing a house with Rodney (*GB*, 205, 215, 223). In other words, she is much the same Wilmet that she has always been.

In Austen's world, a rebuke from Mr Knightley and a discovery of the 'blunders, the blindness of her own head and heart' are enough to engender repentance, contrition, and amendment in Emma (*E*, 374–80, 411–12). Austen accepts and dramatizes the traditional Christian steps toward moral growth, although she makes no overt references to that tradition. In Pym's more overtly Christian world, which is also the modern one, a less rational, more symbolic renewal is required. Conversion or a 'change of heart' cannot be brought about merely by a dramatic confrontation with truth, as it is in the work of novelists who preceded Eliot, James and Conrad. Wilmet achieves her final regeneration in a symbolic, unconscious way that would be inconveivable in *Emma*: it occurs at the retreat house through the largely unconscious operations of her powers of observation and imagination. Covert allusions to *Emma*, then, serve in the end to underscore the enormous aesthetic distance—not merely social—between that novel and *A Glass of Blessings*.

Chapter 20 begins with the unregenerate Wilmet—detached and irritable as a consequence of her sense of not belonging in the world she inhabits. We see detachment in Wilmet's pleasure in escaping from Rodney's 'agonised speculations as to where we were going to live' and from the daunting prospect of their holiday alone together. Irritation is evident when she foresees 'that we should be carrying with us a burden

of gratitude, having to exclaim continually about how lucky
we had been' (GB, 224). Wilmet is also irritated by one of
Mary's first remarks about feeling useless at the retreat house:
Wilmet's response is to 'feel guilty' (GB, 225). Her sense of
guilt is closely tied to her sense of alienation from her world.
By the end of the chapter, however, a subtle change appears in
Wilmet's consciousness. The retreat seems to have worked as
it should. As Wilmet watches the conductor of the retreat—an
old priest—handle a swarm of bees, she moves towards a form
of acceptance and Christian love or charity:

> 'Fancy his knowing about bees', I said. 'I can imagine it might be a
> test of saintliness—certainly of patience.'
>   Standing there watching the old man, I amused myself by
> wondering how the St Luke's priests would have dealt with the
> situation. I could not see Father Thames or Father Ransome as
> being very efficient, but I felt that Father Bode might manage it.
>   'They must find the queen, that is the thing', said one of the
> priests, 'then they will follow her to the hive.'
>   I saw him take out a little note book and jot something down. It
> pleased me to think that here in this pagan part of the garden he
> might have found an idea for a sermon. (GB, 232–3)

She is still a recognizable Wilmet, observant, amused, imaginative. But all these qualities have acquired more charitable
overtones, perhaps because she is more in charity with herself.
The reference to Father Bode—the most Christian character in
the novel—contrasts powerfully with her first references to
him in Chapter 1. There she patronizes 'mild, dumpy little
Father Bode, with his round spectacled face and slightly
common voice', suspecting him of preferring tinned to smoked
salmon, 'though I was ashamed of the unworthy thought for I
knew him to be a good man' (GB, 7). Wilmet's snobbery and
the guilt that usually accompanies it have given way to an
appreciation of Father Bode's and the old priest's virtues—an
appreciation that seems selfless, lacking in jealousy or bitchiness.
    Wilmet's pleasure in detecting common ground between the
pagan garden and a Christian sermon points toward the
largely unconscious processes that have produced renewal in
her. What she observes and imagines within the garden itself

gradually creates in her a kind of acceptance that unites flesh and spirit, paganism and Christianity—and literature. For the humiliation Wilmet brings with her to the garden is very literary. Soon after having discovered that not Piers but Harry gave her the heart-shaped enamel box, she recalls the opening lines of T.S. Eliot's *The Waste Land*. She thus evokes both the bitter despair of the Lenten season and the greater cruelty of renewed hope, symbolized by the 'New Fire of Easter' in the spring (*GB*, 148). Here the explicit allusion to a great English poet—one whom Pym rarely cites—reinforces references that are frequently made in the novels: to the changing of the seasons and to dramatic events in the liturgical year.[20] In Wilmet's consciousness a mixture of 'memory and desire' painfully transforms what a character in a later novel will call 'the soothing rhythm of the church's year' (*QA*, 73).

Once Wilmet has visited the 'wasteland' where Piers's flat is located and has experienced humiliating revelations, she is prepared for the renewal that begins on her second day at the retreat house (*GB*, 169). A compost heap suggests possibilities for renewal out of decay, partly because its richness suggests both life and literature. Pym's complex allusive art is at its most characteristic in this passage, which describes her throwing the pea pods on the compost heap and recalling Marvell's lines, 'My Vegetable love should grow/Vaster than Empires and more slow'. Her subsequent description of the scene is full of complex images:

> There seemed to be a pagan air about this part of the garden, as if Pan—I imagined him with Keith's face—might at any moment come peering through the leaves. The birds were tame and cheeky, and seemed larger than usual; they came bumping and swooping down, peering at me with their bright insolent eyes, their chirpings louder and more piercing than I had ever heard them. I wondered if people who came here for retreats ever penetrated to this part of the garden. I could imagine the unmarried mothers and the schoolboys here, but not those who were striving to have the right kind of thoughts. Then I noticed that beyond the apple trees there was a group of beehives, and I remembered the old saying about telling things to bees. It seemed that they might be regarded as a kind of primitive confessional. (*GB*, 226)

The lines from 'To His Coy Mistress' offer Wilmet a kind of consolation for the loss of her fantasies about Piers—but the consolations of literature in Pym's novels are usually a bit inadequate, even ridiculous. Marvell's lines, in the context of the whole poem (and the novel), are both. They present an absurd image of unconsummated sexual love contrasting both poignantly and comically with the vision that immediately occurs to Wilmet of 'Pan . . . with Keith's face . . . peering through the leaves'.

The lines, the garden, the apple trees, the freedom from labour, the 'richness decaying' and the 'new life', 'Pan', the 'pagan air', and the birds that 'seemed larger than usual'—for Wilmet, these observed, imagined and remembered details register a kind of intensification of life, drawing on natural, pagan, sexual and even biblical imagery. Wilmet then amusingly reflects that the images she has conjured up around Marvell's lines might not suit 'those who were striving to have the right kind of thoughts' (though they might suit the more luxuriant sexuality of 'unmarried mothers and . . . schoolboys'), but the notion of 'telling things to bees' immediately reminds her that natural, pagan, sexual and Christian imagery *can* unite in a 'primitive confessional' (*GB*, 226). That is, she returns to a perception of possible unity, a sense in which the Church, as she has earlier felt, 'should be the place where all worlds could meet. . . . If people remained outside it was our—even *my*—duty to bring them in' (*GB*, 209). In Chapter 20, Wilmet's imagination and observation, operating in the highly symbolic garden of the retreat house, bring all her worlds together.[21]

At the end of the next day, after Wilmet undergoes a final humiliating revelation—that Mary Beamish will marry Marius—the natural, sexual and pagan images come together again in her mind, but the church and Christianity seem absent for the moment:

Sybil and Professor Root, Piers and Keith, Marius and Mary—the names *did* sound odd together—all doing things without, as it were, consulting me. And now Rodney and I would have to set up house on our own, a curious and rather disconcerting thought. I tried to remember our time in Italy, but all that came into my mind

were curious irrelevant little pictures—a dish of tangerines with
the leaves still on them; the immovable shape of Rodney's driver
as we held hands in the back of some strange army vehicle on our
way home from a dance; the dark secret face of a Neopolitan boy
who used to come to stoke the fire in winter; then Keith's face
peering through leaves, one hand resting lightly on the low bough
of an orange tree; and a comfortable looking woman, using
number 11 needles and commencing by casting on 64 stitches . . .
(*GB*, 230)

Here Wilmet's images become increasingly phantasmagoric,
ending with a covert allusion to one of the Fates. The ellipsis
indicates that she falls asleep; any subsequent change in her
occurs unconsciously. Wilmet then wakes in sunlight (openly
suggestive of enlightenment), helps Mary to prepare for the
arrival of priests for the retreat, lazes in a deckchair and, when
the priests come, walks 'among the vegetables' (*GB*, 231).
There she is approached by a village woman asking for help
with the swarming bees. What has happened to Wilmet by this
point is not precisely specified, unless it is hinted in the line that
the priest apparently jots down as a note for a sermon: ' "They
[the bees] must find the queen . . . then they will follow her to
the hive." ' Something central and essential, having been lost,
must first be recognized and then followed or joined, a process
here aided by the 'conductor of the retreat'. This lost quality or
principle is not defined, but it clearly combines pagan, natural,
sexual and Christian elements—and happens to be represented here by something female, a queen bee. Perhaps it is the
Church, understood in the largest possible sense.

In any case, what Wilmet has found does give her '*Victory
over Pan*'. The title, earlier misread by Sybil, becomes
appropriate at last to Wilmet's story (*GB*, 23). She has
achieved a victory that incorporates into her life Pan or Keith
and all he represents of her own errors and her unfulfilled
longings. This victory or renewal allows her to be more
charitable to herself and others. In the chapters that follow
Wilmet's retreat, the renewal she has undergone there is
generally sustained, though not invariably, as is the complex
imagery of regeneration in the garden. The coffee bar where
Keith works, with its fairy-tale name (the Cenerentola, or
Cinderella) reminds her of the compost heap at the retreat—it

is full of the richness of 'the fresh bloom of youth' and sexuality or new life (*GB*, 234).[22] Wilmet is surrounded by 'groups of young people glimpsed dimly through the greenery' (*GB*, 238). Mary's furniture comes well out of the depository, without 'the dramatic decay, the baroque horror' of Wilmet's and Piers's 'wild imaginings' (*GB*, 253). The Church is present too. The name of the coffee house echoes that of the Italian villa where Father Thames will retire, and the church and the coffee bar are more intimately connected in Wilmet's notion that 'Here in the Cenerentola, its hissing coffee machine tended by two handsome young men who seemed as devout as any acolytes, it would not be inappropriate to speak of church and clergy house matters' (*GB*, 212, 237). Paganism is also included: the ceremony that unites the aptly named Sybil and the equally well-named Professor Root in marriage is pagan (*GB*, 234).

Pym's interest in yoking disparate worlds in Chapter 20 of *A Glass of Blessings*, in symbolically uniting Christian with pagan, sexual and natural imagery, may suggest the novels of E.M. Forster to some readers, although Forster is less frequently inclined to admit Christian imagery.[23] But Pym is probably not alluding covertly to Forster. Favourite authors and works tend to recur in Pym's allusions; they form part of her intellectual landscape and present themselves frequently in the novels. So far, however, I have found no overt allusions to Forster's novels in any of her works, published or unpublished. In any case, Pym and Forster take quite different views of Pan. Forster evokes paganism to exalt sexuality and to exorcise the repressions enforced by social convention; Pym approaches sexual expression and repression more humorously throughout her works. For example, Chapter 20, along with the more heavy symbolic freight already discussed, carries a lighter load of a favourite comic metaphor: the one that unites sex and food. This metaphorical equation in Pym's novels, brilliantly expounded in a talk by Victoria Glendinning,[24] and briefly noted earlier by Nardin,[25] suggests that sex and food, two worlds generally thought to be disparate, can in fact be hilariously confused and conflated.

An equation between food and sex is ubiquitous in *A Glass of Blessings*. Perhaps it is clearest when Wilmet has lunch with

Harry, and 'great joints were wheeled up to the table':

> When the joint came to us I found myself turning aside with a kind
> of womanly delicacy, hardly able to look it in the face, for there
> was something almost indecent about the sight of meat in such
> abundance. All the same it was very splendid beef and I found
> myself eating it with enjoyment, even relish. (GB, 88)

Both Wilmet's 'relish' and her 'womanly delicacy' are clearly
excited by sexuality. Earlier, at the sight of a 'spectacled youth
in a raincoat' leafing through a book 'with a faintly porno-
graphic title', Wilmet had 'turned away with what I suppose
was a kind of womanly delicacy' (GB, 24). The sexual implications of Wilmet's relish of meat with Harry, both in this lunch
and in thoughts of other lunches, contrast wonderfully with
the ascetic asexuality of the 'harmless' meal Wilmet chooses
with Sybil at a hideous cafeteria and with the luxurious,
self-caressing quality of 'Wilmet's wanderings' through
grocery stores looking for expensive delicacies (GB, 215–16,
22, 179). All these metaphoric equations between food and
sex reach an appropriate climax in Wilmet's and Rodney's
confessions to each other of 'lunches' with Harry and Piers and
the rather more suggestive 'dinners' with Prudence (GB, 249–
50).

In a sense, choice of food suggests not simply the comic
expression of one's sexuality but larger, more painful issues
concerning the choices life presents, its rewards and disappointments. Love is the most tremendous choice, so
tremendous that Wilmet is relieved to sign a letter to Piers
' "with love", for it gave me a perverse kind of pleasure to
think that love could be no more than a harmless and conventional thing' (GB, 187). Harmless love is like a harmless meal
at a cafeteria, bland, safe, sexless. Although Piers's rival
Portugese teacher tells his class that they ' "must not use the
verb *desejar* [desire] if you are just wanting a glass of water or a
piece of chocolate" ', in fact in this novel desires for rich food,
sex and love all merge (GB, 129). And, like other imagery in
the novel, images of desire come together in Chapter 20. They
are comically fused (though poignantly as well) in the allusion
to Marvell's 'vegetable love' that, incongruously enough, goes

'jingling' through Wilmet's head (*GB*, 226).

Although the context of Marvell's 'vegetable love' suggests the absurdity of a love that increases without climax, a love that remains unconsummated, the image of a vast growing vegetable incorporates another kind of absurdity—more hilarious and perhaps in Pym's context not altogether removed from crude phallic humour. After all, the allusion arises from a compost heap, from something actually generating 'new life'; Marvell's hypothetical image of endless, fruitless lovemaking is not relevant here. The rich garden imagery of Chapter 20 transforms the sluggish, slow, unpassionate 'vegetable love' of the seduction poem into something calm yet lush and fruitful. This transformation seems to have been part of Pym's earliest conception for *A Glass of Blessings*; the manuscript records observations she made on a weekend in the country, most of which find their way into the description of the garden:

Oswestry—lovely hot weekend July 9th–10th

I go to stay with a woman friend, perhaps now liberated from her mother.

Peas go on the compost heap—in the fragrant green twilight under the apple trees, the piles of cut grass, pea pods, etc.

It seemed wanton to be lying in a deckchair before lunch, while she was working [?], so I took an upright canvas chair a [*sic*] sat on the green painted iron seat—or a hard wooden one—like those given in memory of someone—

To visit an old house—like Aston Hall—now a girls school—fine cedars and beech trees—on the lawns. Inside the beautiful (? Adam or similar) fireplaces of white and dark green or grey marble.

My vegetable love should grow
Vaster than Empires and more slow

Birds are tame and cheeky—larger than life—blackbirds and thrushes come bumping and swooping—their songs seem louder and more aggressive. (MS PYM 17, f. 5)

'Vegetable love' becomes another emblem in Chapter 20 of the ways in which apparently disparate worlds like sex and food can unite in the imagination, producing an intensified ('larger than life') but serene appreciation of the rich, various mixture life offers to our observation—even in a compost heap. This love represents a comic formulation of the charity or acceptance that Wilmet assimilates in the chapter.

Charity and acceptance cause renewal not only in Wilmet herself but in her relations to others. She and Piers can share 'agonized amusement' at Bason's line, 'Celibacy of the clergy has always been *our* motto' (*GB*, 237). She is amused by Keith and Bason in the coffee bar and Marius later, but her comments tend to be forebearing or charitable. She reassures Marius that he will be able to do good with Mary's money; and she has 'really grown quite fond of' Keith (*GB*, 242, 247). Above all, Wilmet and Rodney have been brought 'closer together than we had been for years' by their search for a flat, a closeness that finally issues in their mutual laughter over the thought of Prudence Bates' uncomfortable Regency sofa; perhaps they are both thinking of Prudence and Rodney cavorting uncomfortably there (*GB*, 247, 250). The novel ends with Wilmet and Rodney having dinner with Sybil and her husband: 'It seemed a happy and suitable ending to a good day' (*GB*, 256).

'Suitable' is especially significant. The opening chapter of *A Glass of Blessings* emphasizes Wilmet's sense of unsuitability. Her alienation from her world is expressed in everything from the 'unsuitable' ringing of the telephone in church to her 'unsuitable detachment' in voicing the idea that Miss Pim might be in love with Rodney (*GB*, 5, 18).[26] In general, no other Pym work strikes such a quietly positive note in its last sentence.[27] Words like 'happy' and 'good' might almost persuade us that we had reached the end of an Austen novel, if Pym had not chosen to underline the differences between the literary worlds of *A Glass of Blessings* and *Emma*. These differences arise primarily from Pym's symbolic approach to evoking a unifying love or charity—very unlike Austen's final assertion of 'the perfect happiness of the union'—and from a sophisticated art of overt and covert allusion that adds several layers of rich implication to her novel (*E*, 484).

The renewal that dispels alienation and makes a rapprochement with Rodney possible also allows Wilmet to develop a sense of the richness of her own life. This is the happiest ending that Pym's novels afford: the recognition that one's own life, even with its deeper longings unfulfilled, is happier than one had thought. In Wilmet's case, this appreciation extends even to marriage, but she values also her friendships (with women and men), her role in the Church and her relation to Sybil—in many ways, the most attractive relation in the novel. Recognizing the richness of their own lives gives Pym's characters a sense of possibility as well as contentment—a sense that perhaps some changes can be made that will make their lives even richer. What they must always learn first, however, is to appreciate what they already have.

Notes

1. This phrase occurs throughout the novel and throughout Pym's other works. The Judgment Day sermon is reported on pp. 108–12 in *Some Tame Gazelle*.
2. All citations of Austen's fiction will be made in parentheses within the text and are taken from the edition of R.W. Chapman, 5 vols, 3rd edn (Oxford, 1933). When appropriate, the following abbreviation applies: E—*Emma*.
3. An exception is *The Sweet Dove Died*, whose allusion to *Pride and Prejudice* already quoted is covert.
4. *Excellent Women* also alludes in plot, theme and characterization to an earlier novel, *Jane Eyre*, offering almost a rewritten version of the work; see Janice Rossen's essay in this volume. The explicit reference to *Jane Eyre* at the start of the novel, however, means that *Excellent Women* does not rely entirely on covert allusion, as does *A Glass of Blessings*.

   Superficially, *Some Tame Gazelle* may also seem at first to resemble *A Glass of Blessings* in its use of allusion. It appears to draw upon Austen's *Sense and Sensibility* for its structure yet makes no overt allusions to Austen. In fact, however, a structure based upon 'The contrasting personalities of the two sisters', as Pym puts it in her original draft of a blurb, is extremely conventional in the English novel (MS PYM 40, f. 14). All subsequent citations of Pym archival material will appear within parentheses in the text. I am grateful to Hilary Pym and Hazel Holt and to the Bodleian Library for permission to quote from this material, and to Colin Harris for his assistance in using it.
5. David Kubal, 'Fiction Chronicle', *The Hudson Review* 33 (1980): 438. Other recent critics who briefly mention parallels between characters in the two novels include Robert Emmet Long, *Barbara Pym* (New York: Ungar, 1986), pp. 117–18, and Jane Nardin, *Barbara Pym* (Boston: Twayne Publishers, 1985), pp. 108–9.
6. Quoted by J.E. Austen-Leigh, *Memoir of Jane Austen*, ed. R.W. Chap-

man (1926; rpt Oxford: Clarendon Press, 1967), p. 157.
7. Nardin, p. 108. Nardin cites a conversation with Hazel Holt in 1982 as the source for this statement.
8. I would like to thank Hazel Holt for clarifying these comparisons for me in 1987, in a letter dated 1 January, and in conversation. I am also very grateful to her for suggesting the parallel importance of class distinctions in *Emma* and *A Glass of Blessings*.
9. Diana Benet, in her valuable study, *Something to Love: Barbara Pym's Novels* (Columbia: University of Missouri Press, 1986) calls this quality of Wilmet's imagination 'alienating' (p. 81) and offers a persuasive analysis of the complexity of Wilmet's imagination.
10. *The Pleasure of Miss Pym* (Austin: University of Texas Press, 1987), p. 40.
11. In the final version of Chapter 2, Mrs Beamish is 'selfish' and moneyed (*GB*, 19); Sybil remarks, ' "It isn't as if Ella Beamish really needed her—she has plenty of money and could get a paid companion who would expect to be bullied" ' (*GB*, 22). These details are absent from pages 25 and 29 of the original manuscript. There Mrs Beamish is also said to be 'over eighty' (f. 27); in the novel she is 'over seventy', and therefore less obviously in need of her daughter's attendance (*GB*, 20).
12. In notes for a revision of *Some Tame Gazelle* made in the 1940s, Pym notes, 'Go over^all^the characters and make them *worse*—as Proust did' (MS PYM 3, f. 1; here and elsewhere, carets [^]indicate that Pym added words above the line). In a talk on 'The Novelists [*sic*] Voice', produced over thirty years later, after the publication of *Quartet in Autumn*, she indicates that this strategy may have become habitual. She writes, 'Perhaps I have been influenced by something I was once told about Proust—that he was said to go over all his characters and make them worse' (MS PYM 96, f. 104).

'Worse' is ambiguous. Sybil, perhaps the most appealing character in *A Glass of Blessings* is 'worse' in the final version, but all these changes—making her more outspoken, more gritty—render her more attractive. Pym adds such wonderful details as her 'grimly and without enjoyment' trying to arrange flowers, 'tweaking them here and there with impatient gestures', and her statement that 'there seems to be something evil and malicious about chrysanthemums' (*GB*, 10–11). In the novel, Sybil is also somewhat more feminist. In the manuscript, she is 'not sure that I approve of career women, anyway' (f. 23), while in the novel she laughs at the notion that a son is best, pokes fun at the men's 'manly conversation' over their port and suggests that Wilmet should have 'some intellectual occupation' (*GB*, 13, 16, 17).
13. In the manuscript, Mary is said to come away from donating blood 'a little sooner than I ought to have done' in order to arrive at the Settlement meeting on time (MS PYM 17, f. 25); in the novel, she leaves only 'a little sooner than I usually do' (*GB*, 19). Her martyrdom is less sought. Similarly, in the manuscript, Mary replies to Wilmet's rather nasty comment that 'It must be quite exhausting losing all that blood' by asserting that 'it's great fun really' (f. 28); in the novel, Wilmet mentions

the possibility of giving blood herself, and Mary replies, ' "Oh, that's great fun" ' (*GB*, 21). Again, Mary is slightly less the ostentatious martyr.

14. The clergy house and its occupants take an even more prominent place in Pym's notes on the next leaf of the manuscript:

> The plot—a fashionable church (which has lunch hour services)—a vicar and two curates, living in clergy house. All celibates. Then one gets married—the other is rather smug. His wife is 'unsuitable'—he is instituted in a suburban parish—here we could have the induction service—perhaps my own parish—and his wife leaves him or goes off with somebody else.
>
> One part is set on the Riviera—where the vicar, perhaps, takes a party from his parish as he takes over the chaplaincy for some time. An elderly lady living there—in fact a ready made 'Rock' and some unpleasantness between them and the one the vicar brings with him. Do we live in a villa or in a hotel. The resident chaplain longs for his green wet English holiday. . . .
>
> Possible Plan
> Part I—In London   Part II   On the Riviera   Part III Back again
> ?Prefixed with quotations. (MS PYM 17, f. 2)

15. The third-person passages can be found in MS PYM 17, f. 14–20; the first person is restored in MS PYM 17, f. 21. These sections appear in what was originally a second chapter, containing Wilmet's birthday dinner at home with Sybil, Rodney and a guest—William Caldicote of *Excellent Women* in 'The Lime Tree Bower', James Cash in *A Glass of Blessings*. Pym's tendency to 'cannibalize' her earlier works for appropriate characters is well known; she herself explained to Philip Larkin, 'It can be a tiresome affectation. With me it's sometimes laziness—if I need a casual clergyman or anthropologist I just take one from an earlier book' (*VPE*, 203). Lady Nollard, visible in 'The Lime Tree Bower' (f. 25) and in *A Glass of Blessings* as well (*GB*, 19–21), is taken from an unfinished novel drafted in 1939, 'Amanda Wraye' (MS PYM 8, f. 53 and elsewhere).

More interesting than this intertextuality in the conception of characters is the apparent interchangeability of their talk. Some lines that were originally Sybil's in 'The Lime Tree Bower'—on combining marriage with a career and on expecting great things of people only until they are 30 (ff. 17, 22)—are assigned to Wilmet in the novel (*GB*, 11, 16). Some lines or reflections originally Wilmet's become Sybil's, particularly those on labelling people unsatisfactory (MS PYM 17, f. 22; *GB*, 16). Even lines first given to William Caldicote/James Cash, on advertising for assistant priests with 'tempting titbits', a thought that suggests the sad possibility of 'opportunities for youth work' leading to homosexuality (f. 21), are transferred to Sybil in *A Glass of Blessings* (*GB*, 15). One of the most cogent criticisms of Pym's work is that her characters have all the same consciousness. Certainly the characters resemble one another in their tendencies to observe and to imagine, particularly humourous details. Yet they do not have the same histories or biases. A study should be made of instances of apparently 'interchangeable' speeches to determine how interchangeable they are in fact. In these instances from *A Glass of Blessings*, Pym is clearly engaged in the process of differentiating her characters. Once the characters are formed, their speeches cannot be exchanged.

16. Unfortunately, it is impossible to discuss in detail all Pym's overt allusions, even in *A Glass of Blessings*, which is generally less allusive than the works that precede it. The novel is full of references to writers as diverse as W.S. Gilbert (*GB*, 24), Virginia Woolf (*GB*, 78), Elizabeth Gaskell (*Cranford*, *GB*, 106). It is particularly full of references to Pym's own works, even Catherine Oliphant's story 'Sunday Morning', not yet written in *Less than Angels* but certainly conceived (*GB*, 152). The most interesting of the allusions I have not been able to discuss is the one to Wordsworth's lines (*GB*, 242). Its relation to the resolution of *A Glass of Blessings* is especially complex.

17. See an essay apparently written for *The New Review*, MS PYM 98, f. 84.

18. The Wilmet of the manuscript, however, is more assured than her counterpart in the novel. In a cancelled section of an early part of 'The Lime Tree Bower', Wilmet works in an office with Piers and seems more confident and in control than she does in the finished novel: 'I had taken the job because I wanted something to occupy my mind, and to see those odd corners of life which interest me so much more than the obviously attractive ones—the world of printers' readers, the home life of the civil servant—I knew about these now for I had married one of the latter. The closed door of the clergy house ˆstillˆ remained to be stormed' (MS PYM 17, ff. 11–12). In the novel, however, Wilmet seems less sure of herself (though more so than any Pym heroine other than Prudence Bates or Leonora Eyre), and not simply because she feels vaguely uneasy about her jobless and childless position. She certainly does not 'storm' the clergy house. Again, she finds that she needs Mary Beamish to introduce her into the 'charmed circle' of church decorators.

19. Nardin, p. 109.

20. Although the Archdeacon quotes Eliot in the second part of his Judgment Day sermon, neither Belinda nor the reader hears it (**STG**, 118). Earlier, Belinda recognized that none but a 'modern poet . . . Eliot perhaps' could do justice to the presence of a caterpillar in cauliflower cheese (*STG*, 51). The only other references that I have found to Eliot occur in *Crampton Hodnet* (Stephen Latimer, rejected by Miss Morrow, thinks of the final lines of *The Waste Land* [*CH*, 96]) and in *A Few Green Leaves* (Emma Howick reads Eliot [*FGL*, 165]).

21. Long offers a parallel interpretation of this chapter and the ones that surround it in *Barbara Pym*, pp. 123–6. He feels, however, that Pym is suggesting an 'interpenetration' between 'the Christian and the pagan', the 'religious and the secular' (p. 123). His view is traditionally Christian; Wilmet must symbolically confess her guilt in Chapter 20 in

order to begin a 'new life' (p. 124). I consider that Pym's imagery achieves something more complex: the rendering of a partially unconscious process of renewal through a combination of observation and imagination. The emphasis is on acquiring charity rather than confessing guilt. In effect, charity casts out guilt. This process of acquiring charity embraces traditional Christianity, but not in a traditional manner.

22. Long has pointed out some of the implications of this imagery of 'new life' in his analysis of Chapter 21 (pp. 124–5). Again, his emphasis is on union of the religious and the secular.

23. Virginia Hjelmaa has thoroughly studied Forster's own art of overt and covert allusion in a dissertation on 'E.M. Forster's Fictional Sources: A Study of the Edwardian Novels' (University of Newcastle upon Tyne, 1983). Her discussion of the complexities created by covert allusions in novels is very helpful.

24. The talk, entitled 'The Pym Man', was given on 5 July 1986, at the Barbara Pym Conference held at St Hilda's College, Oxford. Glendinning rightly pointed out that sex and desire are continually talked about in Pym's novels, via displacement onto food and even woollen goods. She noted, for example, that wives tend to give husbands poor food in the novels, and that the caterpillar found by Miss Prior in her cauliflower cheese in *Some Tame Gazelle* is the best example—that is, the funniest—of male sexuality in the early novels. Amusingly, the manuscript of *A Glass of Blessings* includes a parallel moment: Wilmet finds a slug in her lettuce when Sybil takes her to a seedy cafeteria (MS PYM 17, f. 30). In the novel, Wilmet is simply fearful of 'grit and live things' (*GB*, 23).

25. Nardin points out that the phrase 'cooking his meat' in *Excellent Women* 'seems to have comic sexual overtones' (p. 81).

26. Pym seems to have added the emphasis on 'unsuitability'. Although the ringing of the telephone and Rodney's nickname 'Noddy' are described as 'unsuitable' both in the manuscript of *A Glass of Blessings* and the final version, three occurrences of 'unsuitable' were added to what became the first chapter of the novel before it was published. Apart from 'unsuitable detachment', they include Sybil's sarcastic remark that 'male conversation' is thought to be 'unsuitable' for women and Wilmet's notion that to speak of going to the Settlement as 'amusing' would be 'unsuitable' (*GB*, 16, 18).

27. Perhaps *A Few Green Leaves* comes closest in its last line, with Emma's thought of a not necessarily 'unhappy' love affair with Tom. A more rapturous rather than quietly positive note is struck at the end of *Some Tame Gazelle*, when Belinda is 'overjoyed' by the new curate's appropriateness for Harriet, and other novels mention 'richness' or 'infinite possibilities for change' (*Jane and Prudence* and *Quartet in Autumn*).

Chapter 8

On Not Being Jane Eyre: The Romantic Heroine in Barbara Pym's Novels

JANICE ROSSEN

'Let me hasten to add that I am not at all like Jane Eyre, who must have given hope to so many plain women who tell their stories in the first person, nor have I ever thought of myself as being like her' (*EW*, 7). Thus declares Mildred Lathbury early in Barbara Pym's *Excellent Women*, and the disclaimer is typical of Mildred's modesty and wit. It is also deliberately misleading. If a romantic heroine is one who can fall passionately in love, both Jane Eyre and Mildred Lathbury qualify for the role, and Mildred is not as unlike Jane as she claims to be. They are both unconventional romantic heroines in being 'plain' rather than beautiful, yet they both suffer for love. And Mildred clearly sees herself, however satirically, in this tradition. Many of Pym's other works show traces of Brontë's Victorian novel. References to *Jane Eyre* throughout her writing career and in various contexts suggest that the novel continued to inspire—or to haunt her.[1] She wrote to Philip Larkin in 1969, 'I get comfort from a re-reading of Anthony Powell and Charlotte Brontë (not *Jane Eyre*)' (*VPE*, 248). The disquieting lack of comfort she finds in Brontë's novel becomes transformed in Pym's own fiction into a study of alternative renderings of the Jane Eyre story, as she rewrites *Jane Eyre* in at least three different variations.

Numerous other novels influenced her work as well, as one would expect. Pym drew from a variety of literary sources, sprinkling her novels and short stories with quotations from poetry and with allusions to characters in other fiction. Nor is she unique as a writer in this tendency to look to the past. Feminist critics have convincingly illustrated the almost over-powering influence which Victorian women writers in particular have exerted on their twentieth-century counterparts.[2] Still, a comparison between Pym and Brontë's fiction yields more than simply another example of recurrent Victorian influence. Pym consciously modelled her work on Brontë's in order to mark her own identification with the frustrations which Brontë depicts as inherent in a woman's lot—or, more broadly, both writers address the theme of confronting disappointment and hardship. Thus *Jane Eyre* forms a paradigm for three of Pym's novels, widely separated in time: *Something to Remember* (unpublished, begun 1940), *Excellent Women* (1952) and *The Sweet Dove Died* (1978). Set in this framework, the novels' plots can be seen to echo Brontë's by focusing on the aspect of renunciation of passion and romance through moral strength of will. Pym's novels avoid the dramatic overtones of Brontë's gothic tale, but they explore the same issues with an acute consciousness of this literary background behind them.

Pym's heroines are often like Jane Eyre in their social position as embryo 'distressed gentlewomen'. They also share her conviction that love is not to be expected for them, although they each embrace unrequited love as their fate, worshipping some unattainable, glamourous man from afar. At the same time, *not* being 'like Jane Eyre' for Pym's heroines results in the fact that they ultimately succeed in renouncing their love for the Rochester heroes. In Brontë's novel, Jane must do this twice: once when she feels herself initially attracted to Rochester during her term as governess, while he is courting Blanche Ingram, and later when she flees Thornfield after Rochester attempts to marry her bigamously. This renunciation of her lover is meant to seem admirable to the reader, and in narrating the story Jane stresses the compelling rightness of her decisions not to hope for his love and to leave him. Yet, as critics have pointed out, the moral aspect of the tale is undermined by the novel's resolution: romantic love triumphs in Jane's reunion with Rochester. The heroine need not, in the end, give the hero up at all.

For Pym's heroines, the problem of renouncing their love

takes less overtly dramatic forms, but remains no less urgent. The same process of emotionally tearing away from an adored object of affection occurs inevitably for them as well. They must renounce hope of uniting with their Rochester heroes, and as a result they grieve silently for their loss. Their bitterness is compounded by the fact that they feel humiliated by the consciousness that they are not loved in return. Unlike Jane Eyre, who is loved passionately although she is not beautiful, Mildred Lathbury can give no hope to 'plain women'.

The test of successfully renounced passion does not lie in whether the heroine refuses to marry the hero, as in a conventional romantic resolution, but in what she does instead. Pym's novels offer studies in precisely this subject: renunciation of the romantic hero by substituting something else. They are 'how to' books on falling out of love. Each of the heroines in *Something to Remember, Excellent Women* and *The Sweet Dove Died* must struggle to renounce her passion. None possesses Jane Eyre's scope, chances or character, although they each compare themselves directly to this Victorian heroine; individually, each lacks her fire and verve. Pym chooses a drawing-room mode for her contemporary novels rather than the gothic genre which infuses Brontë's Victorian novel. Yet in addressing the same issues, she reflects and revises the *Jane Eyre* tradition by altering the ending of the story. And this results in its own peculiar lack of comfort in each of the three modernized versions of Brontë's tale.

The unfinished fragment *Something to Remember* seems to be clearly modelled on *Jane Eyre*. The novel is narrated by a plain spinster named Deborah Wilde, a heroine who is palpably like Jane Eyre in her similar social position: where Jane goes from Lowood girls' school to a 'new servitude' as governess at Thornfield Hall, Deborah takes up a new post in London at the Otways' house, where she will be a secretary and lady's companion to Mrs Otway. The novel opens with Deborah's preparations for this change, and much of the opening chapters concerns Deborah's fears about settling into the new house and living among new people. She is self-conscious because of her subservient position, wondering if she 'should be miserable and unable to do anything right'. She goes on to generalize about gentlewomen in her position, who are, she infers, 'ill-treated and put upon'. The source for these anxieties is not surprising: she confides, 'I remembered the novels of Charlotte Brontë' (MS PYM 11, f. 24). Yet as though to mock the seriousness of Brontë's novel, sinister overtones in Pym's setting soon become dispelled in comic antics. Far from discovering a madwoman in the attic, Deborah lives there comfortably herself; and she finds the most unusual aspect of the house to be a huge number of stuffed birds, dusty and harmless relics of the Victorian age. Her employers are considerate, if mildly eccentric, and the maid treats her like she is a lady.

The situation is deliberately anachronistic, and almost certainly reflects an attempt to create a contemporary version of *Jane Eyre*. As this early novel bears on the plight of a gentlewoman going out to work for a living, the plot is contrived and the setting artificial. The house in Belgrave Square is no Thornfield Hall. Yet as the novel progresses, Deborah reveals that this particular setting is incidental to the main theme: renunciation of a lost love. Deborah has previously been jilted for another woman by the Rev. Bernard Hoad, one of her father's curates—for she also, like Jane Eyre, has been a clergyman's daughter and is now an orphan. With the introduction of this issue, the plot suddenly comes into focus. The story is that of *Jane Eyre* slightly misplaced, where the heroine comes to a new house in order to escape passion and feeling, not to find an outlet for it. Her position in the Otways' house makes Deborah Wilde into a Jane Eyre governess figure, and her grieving for her former fiancé allies her with Jane Eyre the romantic heroine. Both women mourn lost loves. Thus Deborah's story recreates Jane Eyre's period of mourning after the rupture of her marriage with Rochester.

As Deborah Wilde shows traces of the Jane Eyre character, the absent hero of the tale shows affinities with Brontë's male characters, though in a comic mode. His name, Bernard Hoad, suggests a cross between a hoax and a toad, and he unites aspects of the two heroes in *Jane Eyre*. Like Rochester, he has been a deeply romantic figure for Deborah. At the same time, in terms of his profession he also represents the clergyman figure of Brontë's St John, the man with an exalted mission whom Deborah could have 'helped' in his work. She would have been so '*suitable*' as a clergyman's wife, as Mrs Otway stresses, after she hears the story of the broken engagement (MS PYM 11, f. 69). As Bernard assumes dual roles of lover and of clergyman, Deborah also is rejected twice over in two roles, both as the woman who is loved for herself alone and as the helpmeet who is useful. In Pym's novel the hero rejects the heroine rather than pursuing her, as Rochester and St John pursue Jane Eyre. Still, the problem of renouncing passion once it becomes untenable remains the same for both heroines.

This is further reinforced by the cautionary example of yet another Jane Eyre figure, Miss Mower, who is Deborah's predecessor as companion to Mrs Otway. At the end of the novel, Deborah learns why Miss Mower had left the post which Deborah now fills: she had fallen in love with Mr Otway. Overcome by excessive emotion, Miss Mower had fled from London to her sister's house in Cambridge and there died of pneumonia (if not of a broken heart). Miss Mower's flight represents one possible response to hopeless love. Her story affects Deborah profoundly, as she too attempts to recover from one actual rejection (by Bernard Hoad) and from another potential one (by Mr Otway, assuming she were to follow Miss Mower's example and develop a passion for him). Curiously, Deborah contemplates the possibility of falling in love with Mr Otway—an old, dried-up politician, and no vigorous Rochester—as an *ersatz* preventive against the genuinely romantic love she cherished for Bernard Hoad. With such a shrivelled object of devotion as Mr Otway, her hypothetical love would be so remote as to be 'soothing': 'It made me feel safe', she confesses, 'as if I were at last free from all the miseries that a flesh and blood passion can bring with it' (MS PYM 11, f. 68–9).

Through these connections with *Jane Eyre, Something to Remember* attempts to resolve through comedy the problem of the plain woman who is denied love. Mrs Otway giggles as she relates to Deborah the sad history of Miss Mower, and even Deborah cannot repress a smile as she contemplates an example of such extravagant romanticism. In reaction to Miss Mower's example, Deborah Wilde attempts to control her own passion. Her name is ironic in this respect, as Deborah is not wild, although she does attempt the satiric wit of Oscar

Wilde in seeing romantic love in a cynical light. The novel labours to show that the modern romantic heroine can renounce love by substituting artifice in the form of a 'soothing' distant passion or by substituting art itself, thus illustrating a Wildean aesthetic tenet. Deborah bears Bernard's rejection bravely by cherishing his Christmas gift of the *Oxford Book of English Verse*. 'He took away himself but left with me the great English poets instead', she confides, 'and after a while they began to be a consolation, as they always had been' (MS PYM 11, f. 46).

This early novel is a strange combination of heavy moral satire at Miss Mower's expense and of Deborah's half-serious attempts to abandon passion altogether. Deborah both does and does not want to see herself as a Jane Eyre heroine who falls in love, as Miss Mower has done earlier in her place. Although it attempts to brush aside the devastation that unrequited love can bring, the novel strikes an elegiac mood ending on a note of regret for Deborah's lost chance at being a clergyman's wife. Because of the heroine's chronic disappointment in life, comfort maintains its high value, as can be seen in the 'consolation' rendered by English poetry. In the end, it can be made to replace love. Such a resolution to the novel leaves the reader uneasy as to the moral which Pym is suggesting. One is uncertain whether to smile at the heroine's excessive protestations or to nod sagely in agreement with her over the weakness and superficiality of men. Deborah tries to make a joke of her own rejection and of Miss Mower's unfortunate demise. And yet both women have encountered such obvious depths of grief and such terrible consequences from loving that it remains difficult to take the moral lightly. In order to effectively make a comedy of the situation, Pym needed to devise another means of presenting it, which she did in *Excellent Women*.

Where *Something to Remember* retells the aspect of *Jane Eyre* in which the heroine attempts to forget the hero several years after a disappointment, *Excellent Women* shows the evolution of a romantic relationship from its beginning. In a slightly skewed way, the novel recreates the Thornfield Hall episode where Jane and Rochester first meet. Both Mildred and Jane live in the same houses as their romantic heroes, and they share a corresponding ambivalence toward these buildings and their positions there. Jane comes to Thornfield Hall as a dependant and a governess, while Mildred rents a flat in the same building into which Rocky and Helena Napier move early in the novel. Jane first looks to Thornfield as a possible haven which will provide larger scope for her, although she is keenly conscious of her subservient status. On her return from town, for instance, after she has first met Mr Rochester, Jane hesitates outside: 'I did not like re-entering Thornfield. To pass its threshold was to return to stagnation . . . I lingered at the gates; I lingered on the lawn; I paced backwards and forwards on the pavements' and so on.[3] Mildred similarly sees the building which contains her flat as somewhere she doesn't quite have the right to be. She is first introduced to the reader in a similar position of hesitation outside, as she watches her new neighbours' furniture being unloaded and carried through the front door of the building. When a passing churchwarden of her acquaintance accosts her, she starts 'guiltily, almost as if I had no right to be discovered outside my own front door' (EW, 5).

Both heroines are sharp and inquisitive. The churchwarden's prophecy to Mildred proclaimed on the pavement proves to be correct: ' "Ah, you ladies! Always on the spot when there's something happening!" ' (EW, 5). In their position as resident observers, Jane and Mildred discover domestic secrets in their respective dwellings and appear 'on the spot' for important revelations, though in Pym's novels, of course, these are invariably revelations of a slightly absurd nature. In Jane Eyre, Rochester's lunatic wife is revealed to be confined in the attic. In Excellent Women, Mildred herself lives in the flat upstairs from the Napiers (the attic rooms, which comprise part of her flat, are actually empty). Even so, Rockingham Napier's wife is discovered to be mad for her profession of anthropology and for her colleague Everard Bone, with whom she is in love. And Mildred herself falls in love with Rocky, a self-revelation which surprises her—and which causes her continual misery. The domestic mysteries which Mildred uncovers in the course of the novel are an ironic diminution of those Jane confronts in Jane Eyre. While Jane sees Bertha rush at Rochester in a murderous fit of madness,

Mildred learns that Rocky and Helena are unhappy in their marriage, through overhearing such signs of imminent trouble as when Rocky tells his wife, ' "Darling, you are *filthy* . . . putting down a hot greasy frying-pan on the linoleum!" ' (*EW*, 52).

Comic and trivial as these revelations may be, they unmask an important truth: Rocky exerts much the same influence on Mildred that Rochester does on Jane. The two heroes are both notorious rakes and charmers. As Rochester has had his series of international mistresses in Céline, Giacinta and Clara, Rocky Napier has enjoyed a similar harem in the group of Wrens who systematically fell in love with him during his naval duty in Italy. (Less profligate than Rochester, he is only revealed to have kept one mistress, an Italian 'girlfriend' during the Wrens period.) Rochester declares to Jane that he is finally sickened by this procession of courtesans: ' "It was a grovelling fashion of existence" '; he tells her, ' "I should never like to return to it" ' (*JE*, 314). More frivolous altogether, Rocky shows correspondingly less seriousness about the matter. On the subject of romance, he tells Mildred, ' "Once you get into the habit of falling in love you will find that it happens quite often and means less and less" ' (*EW*, 136). Thus as Mildred is a lighter version of Jane, Rocky is a more informal, comic version of Rochester.

Yet at the same time he is also equally attractive to her as Rochester is to Jane. Like Rochester, Rockingham is dark, tempting, profligate and charming. Further, he arouses in Mildred the desire and need to serve him; both Jane and Mildred continually step in to perform domestic duties that the heroes' wives neglect. For example, both men make their first appearances in the novels by arriving at their respective homes after a long journey in foreign lands, and are welcomed by the heroines. Jane helps Rochester to his horse, when he has fallen with a sprained ankle, and Mildred answers Rocky's ring at the front door—Helena is out—and fixes him a cup of coffee. This domestic proximity causes love to develop in roughly the same way in both novels and to be similarly incapable of expression. Though thrown into contact with the heroes continually, neither Mildred nor Jane can reveal her love for Rochester or Rockingham.

The parallels between the two novels are not exact, of course. Rochester does, in fact, love Jane even while he seems to worship Blanche Ingram, whereas Rocky never shows any romantic interest in Mildred. Still, the heroines' need to renounce love for the heroes is the same in both novels. Mildred and Jane must both decide what to do once fulfilment of their passion proves hopeless. And the advent of an alternate hero at this stage in each plot marks the difference in their choices.

A crisis in each novel wrenches the heroines from the men they love. Jane leaves Thornfield when her marriage to Rochester becomes aborted, and Rocky leaves the flat in London and retires to a country cottage when Helena deserts him after a quarrel. At this point in the narratives, a contrasting hero gains increasing importance, in the figures of St John Rivers and Everard Bone. Both are fair, tall and handsome, thus possessing a superficial resemblance to each other. In character, they are also similar: St John is repeatedly described as 'hard', 'icy', and 'cold', adjectives which suit Everard as well. St John is a clergyman, a role which Everard could easily adopt, Mildred thinks, as he would be properly 'forbidding'.

The two men are also fanatically devoted to their respective causes. St John sees missionary work in India as his crusade, while Everard embraces anthropology and studies tribes in Africa. They are both committed scholars, and their severity about their work is equally austere. An example of this occurs early in *Excellent Women*, when Mildred tries to converse with Everard about his profession, which she hazards must be enjoyable, a view he disdains: ' " 'Fun' is hardly the word", he said. "It's very hard work, learning an impossibly difficult language, then endless questionings and statistics, writing up notes and all the rest of it" ' (*EW*, 35). Similarly, St John sees missionary work as his inevitable vocation, stressing the work's increased glory *because* of its attendant hardships. When Jane urges him to abandon it in order to marry Rosamond Oliver, he refuses passionately on the grounds of a personal calling: ' "Relinquish! What! my vocation? My great work? . . . It is dearer than the blood in my veins. It is what I have to look forward to, and to live for" ' (*JE*, 376).

The heroes' seriousness about their work becomes of crucial

importance to Jane and Mildred because it bears directly on
their fate. Since they are each perceived as able assistants in the
work to be undertaken, they are called into action. St John
categorically rejects marrying the beautiful Rosamond because he wants, as he tells Jane, a 'missionary's wife'. With her
gravity and plainness, Jane is the obvious choice. Thus when
he later presses her to marry him, this becomes the major force
of his argument: ' "God and nature intended you for a
missionary's wife" ', he tells her, adding that she is ' "formed
for labour, not for love. A missionary's wife you must—shall
be" ' (*JE*, 405). Everard's call to Mildred to join the ranks of
the anthropologists is hardly less straightforward—and self-
interested. His appeal intends the same effect, that of assuming
that Mildred will help him because she must perceive that she
can be useful. Indeed, when she goes to his flat for dinner in the
final scene of the novel, Mildred is so certain that he will
appeal to her on these grounds that she determines to refuse
any such plea for help. Ironically, of course, her efforts in
hair-style and dress *not* to appear to be a suitable academic
helpmeet are utterly futile. They reveal her to be 'altogether
exactly the kind of person who would be able to correct proofs
or make an index' (*EW*, 248). Unlike Jane Eyre, confused by a
similar situation, Mildred does agree to help the work-
obsessed hero; she ends by volunteering to proofread Everard's scholarly manuscripts. His response illustrates the profoundly impersonal nature of this type of hero; like St John,
Everard is most passionate regarding his work. Her offer of
help makes him ecstatic: 'I had never seen Everard so enthusiastic before', she observes (*EW*, 255).

The clerical help which Mildred envisions giving to Everard
extends in Pym's later novels to their marriage. *Excellent
Women* itself remains open-ended, but Pym's next novel, *Jane
and Prudence*, reveals that the two have married, and that
Mildred has learnt to type as well as to proofread and index.
To further underscore this utilitarian aspect of their relationship, Esther Clovis reflects in retrospect in *Less than
Angels* on Mildred's usefulness as a wife: 'Everard had married a rather dull woman who was nevertheless a great help to
him in his work; as a clergyman's daughter she naturally got
on very well with the missionaries they were meeting now that

they were in Africa again' (*LTA*, 64–5). Thus in these novels Barbara Pym rewrites *Jane Eyre* with a different ending: Mildred must renounce her love for Rocky, and does so by substituting marriage to Everard Bone and the work she can do for him. She goes to Africa with Everard, in the same way that Jane might have gone to India with St John.

As a coda which rounds out the comparison with Brontë's novel, Pym adds a later footnote regarding Rocky's fate as well. His departure to the country cottage echoes Rochester's removal to the remote farmhouse Ferndean, where Jane will eventually find him at the end of *Jane Eyre*. Significantly, Mildred longs to visit Rocky at his cottage but waits in vain for an invitation. The traditional happy ending is ultimately achieved by being displaced onto Rocky's wife, Helena. In Pym's later novel, *A Glass of Blessings*, we learn that part of the *Jane Eyre* story has been fullfilled through Helena's return to her husband. Miserable without him, she at length abandons anthropology, joins Rocky at the cottage and in due course presents him with a child, as Jane does to Rochester.

Pym's rewriting of Brontë's ending might in some ways offer more 'comfort' to the reader if only by avoiding some of the problems which Brontë encounters in contriving her romantic resolution. The conclusion of *Jane Eyre* seems to some readers exasperating in its earnest assurances of connubial bliss. Several critics have found the domestic ménage at Ferndean problematic, as Ferndean itself is alleged by Rochester to be in a damp, unhealthy location. More pressingly, Jane does not ultimately achieve equality with Rochester. Wyatt shrewdly points out that Brontë's heroine ends entirely subsumed in a patriarchal system and withdrawn into passivity.[4] Edwards sees Jane's return to Rochester as constituting a constrictive narrowing of her sphere: 'In rejecting St John's heroism, Jane rejects her own as well . . . she abandons action for love, and the larger world is displaced by an idealized but hermetic domesticity'.[5] On the other hand, a possible marriage with St John would entail more for Jane than a matter of sharing his missionary work in India. She rejects him personally because of his desire to control her; she does not reject the work itself. With a twist of humour one might almost expect from a character in a Pym novel, Jane offers to go abroad with St John as his curate, though not as his wife.

In this alternative rendering of the story through her contemporary characters, Pym suggests that Everard takes Mildred for granted, but not that he crushes her spirit, as St John seeks to do to Jane. The marriage seems workable enough. But the most compelling difference between the two novels is that Pym avoids trying to persuade her readers that the heroine finds a happy romantic ending, and refuses to resolve her plot neatly at the end of the novel. We learn of Mildred's marriage only later and indirectly, through other characters. Thus we have no personal protestations of happiness from Mildred to doubt. She goes out of her way to insist that she is 'not at all like Jane Eyre', while in her own narrative Jane discloses her own fate and her rejoicing in it. Whether Pym's contemporary rendering of the romance creates a better resolution for the heroine is, of course, open to question, but the main interest lies less in the dubious success of such an attempt than in the fact that Pym made the experiment. *Excellent Women* offers a mild, muted, absurd comedy which counterpoints Brontë's intense, introspective novel. While Brontë broke the mold of the comedy of manners, writing a novel of passion and romance, Pym rewrites Brontë's *Jane Eyre* back into a drawing-room mode.

Pym attempts yet another variation of *Jane Eyre* in her novel *The Sweet Dove Died*. The heroine, Leonora Eyre, possesses a doubly romantic name, in a combination which at least one character finds '*disquieting*' (SDD, 85). The name is ironic because, contrary to her literary namesakes, Leonora embodies narcissism rather than bravery or romance. The Leonora of Beethoven's opera *Fidelio* disguises herself as a man in order to enter the jail where her husband has been imprisoned and to free him. In an inversion of this, the Leonora of Pym's novel imprisons rather than frees James, the younger man with whom she falls in love. In addition, the mistaken sexual identity of the disguised Leonora in the opera is paralleled ironically by the confusion caused in the novel by James's bisexuality.

Like her other counterpart, Jane Eyre, Leonora Eyre struggles with her passion for James. In this quasi-romance,

however, she assumes the masculine role of pursuer and
manipulator. In a reversal of arrangements at Thornfield Hall,
Leonora owns the house in this novel, and places James in the
attic above her, literally moving his furniture into the upstairs
flat in her house, while he is away on a trip to the continent.

Passion becomes antithetical to comfort in this novel, and
Leonora fails to keep James in part because of her preference
for one to the other. While in one sense she is the aggressor in
their relationship, she remains reticent on this crucial point.
Leonora does not renounce passion, like Jane Eyre, but seeks
to control or suppress it, both in herself and in the men she
attracts. She creates an aesthetic out of romance. This is most
clearly seen in the difference between the love scenes in Pym's
and Brontë's novels. The Edenic garden in which Jane and
Rochester first passionately confess their mutual love is paralleled by many such episodes for Leonora, who 'had had
romantic experiences in practically all the famous gardens of
Europe, beginning with the Grosser Garten in Dresden where,
as a schoolgirl before the war, she had been picked up by a
White Russian prince' (SDD, 48). She is experienced in romance, but only in terms of these virginal garden encounters.
The narrator concludes that Leonora remains unaffected,
almost 'untouched' by these interludes.

The contrast between the two novels illustrates as much
about the hero of the piece as it does about Leonora. Unlike
Rochester, James is a much diminished romantic figure. Early
in the novel, the two walk in a garden near Leonora's house,
recreating the 'pickings-up' of Leonora's continental career.
But it is all a 'very far cry' from the great gardens of the past
and the noble suitors. James himself resists being there, reflecting that he 'would have preferred to sink into a chair with a
drink at his elbow rather than traipse round the depressing
park with its formal flowerbeds and evil-faced little statue—a
sort of debased Peter Pan—at one end and the dusty grass and
trees at the other' (SDD, 46). Thus James is no romantic hero,
but instead becomes the living representation of the perennial,
effeminate Peter Pan figure who refuses to grow up.

In The Sweet Dove Died, passion becomes a threatening and
powerful force, and Leonora's attempts to alternately avoid or
control it make the novel a parody of a conventional romance.

The hero, and not the heroine, is pursued, and not by Leonora alone. James is seduced by the younger bluestocking, Phoebe, in the attic of Vine Cottage, and later by Ned, in a London flat. These two competitors for James's love succeed, in this sense, where Leonora fails, by avoiding formal gardens and by luring James into wilder settings for romance. Phoebe's country cottage is covered by unruly vines, while Ned's flat suggests an indoor jungle. Ned's flat (which is upstairs, and thus especially appropriate for passion) emanates a cave-like atmosphere: 'A large black rug of synthetic fur covered half the floor and in one corner was a red divan heaped with cushions, also of a fur-like material. The general impression was disturbing in some undefined way' (SDD, 157). On one occasion, Ned shows Leonora his bed, as if to mark James for his own territory; when she inquires 'foolishly' if it is comfortable, he taunts her by replying ' "maybe comfort isn't all I go for" ' (SDD, 157). Ned embraces sex as the unsettling, disquieting element that Leonora strives to avoid. She seeks on the contrary to keep James passive, approving the chaste kiss on cheek or brow which was 'all he seemed to want'. She in turn desires 'comfort' rather than passion.

The absence of sex (which in turn assures cosiness) becomes increasingly sinister as the novel progresses. Comfort in these terms becomes stifling and confining. An example of this occurs midway through the novel, when Leonora takes James to a cat show. He feels menaced by the sexual ambiguity which the animals represent: ' "Just kittens and neuter cats", said Leonora, reading from the programme, "that sounds so cosy, doesn't it?" ' She characteristically feels at home in this milieu, but James's response is apprehensive: ' "Shall I be the only grown-up male thing there, then?" James asked, not altogether joking' (SDD, 65).

One of the caged animals at the cat show illustrates the futility of life which excludes sexual freedom and creates a monk-like, hermetic existence:

> They had stopped in front of a cage where a cat-like shape shrouded in a cloth lay fast asleep. How much wiser to contract out altogether, James felt, as this creature had evidently done. Or to sit stolidly in one's earth tray, unmoved by the comments of

passers-by. Yet too often, like some of the more exotic breeds, one
prowled uneasily round one's cage uttering loud plaintive cries.
(*SDD*, 68)

The novel as a whole plays on this tension: what is one to do
with one's passion? The caged cat echoes Bertha's captivity in
Thornfield Hall, where she too paces back and forth, as does
Jane in moments of agitation. In James's view, one can deny
such needs—'contract out altogether'—or remain conscious
of others yet strive to remain 'unmoved', which is Leonora's
choice. James attempts to escape the cage altogether, 'prowl-
ing' with Leonora, then Phoebe, then Ned.

The novel's conclusion finds Leonora becoming true to both
of her names and reverting to her earlier life, ultimately
'untouched' by James. A minor character has earlier fantasized
about 'the idea of Jane Eyre supervising the packing of Mr
Rochester's furniture', and Leonora fulfils this by gathering
James's things into the flat she has prepared in her house
(*SDD*, p. 86). Yet she also sets him free at the end, or rather,
refuses to invite him back when he returns to her abjectly at the
end of the novel. She will not 'lure' him again into a 'cage',
which she has done before. Thus as 'Leonora', she liberates
James, and as 'Eyre', she has suffered deeply and has renounced her passion for him. Leonora returns to her previous
relations with men, in encounters which are marked by distance and aesthetic elegance. The attic will henceforward
remain empty, since James moves out, though as a compensation the garden episodes will continue: at the close of the
novel, James's uncle, Humphrey, appears at Leonora's front
door with a propitiatory bouquet. Further, the ending of the
novel projects similar outings: 'The sight of Humphrey with
the peonies reminded her that he was taking her to the Chelsea
Flower Show tomorrow' (*SDD*, 208).

The Sweet Dove Died recounts the rise and inevitable fall of
a doomed relationship—the outcome is never in doubt. James
will leave; and Leonora genuinely grieves when he does. But in
the end she is able to renounce him. The significance of this
particular episode is that it questions Leonora's continual
demonstrated preference for cosiness attained through control
and denial of passion. As a romantic heroine, she is not like

Jane Eyre because she rejects passion in favour of formality and distance. This can offer the advantage of insulation from grief; still, it makes even the blessing of comfort appear unattractive.

Though Barbara Pym's fiction has most often been compared to that of Jane Austen, Charlotte Brontë seems to exert a powerful hold over her imagination as well. At the least, the same problems which haunt Brontë's heroine with such gripping force shadow Pym's heroines as well. Though Mildred and Leonora are placed in much more comfortable circumstances, and face no such dramatic confrontations as Jane does in discovering the animalistic Bertha, they too suffer for love. Leonora's momentary disorientation in *The Sweet Dove Died* shows that near madness is possible in Pym's decorous world as well.

Much of Pym's ambivalence about relationships between men and women finds expression in parody and overstatement. One of her most vigorous statements on the nature of men occurs in the novel *Jane and Prudence*, where an elderly spinster, Miss Doggett, proclaims that ' "men only want *one thing*" '. Sex, of course, is what men demand; yet even the authoritative Miss Doggett follows this assertion with seeming puzzlement, as she appears to have 'forgotten for the moment what it was' (*JP*, 70). What, indeed, do men want? Perhaps the main difference between Brontë's and Pym's answer to this question lies in the innate strength of will apparent in their male characters. In *Jane Eyre*, at least, both Rochester and St John know with absolute determination what they desire: ' "man meddle not with me: I have her, and will hold her" ', declares Rochester in defiance of fate, when Jane has agreed to marry him (*JE*, 258). St John's forceful proposals to Jane are no less determined. She 'must and shall' be his wife.

Pym's male characters, by contrast, cannot easily decide. Bernard Hoad of *Something to Remember* carelessly changes brides. Rocky Napier of *Excellent Women* confides to Mildred that perhaps he ought not to have married Helena; even so, he is not sure of this, and compensates by various casual episodes of adultery. Everard Bone is doubtless a kinder version of Brontë's St John, and this makes his marriage to Mildred more acceptable; still, James in *The Sweet Dove Died* is malleable in the extreme. He vacillates even in determining which sex most attracts him.

Gilbert and Gubar have seen *Jane Eyre* as a cross between gothic romance and moral didacticism.[6] Pym rejects the gothic element, dispels sinister overtones and shifts the moral emphasis of Brontë's novel. This is especially apparent in the novels' contrasting endings. Jane Eyre concludes her confessional novel with the testimony of perfect bliss: 'I know what it is to live entirely for and with what I love best on earth', she affirms (*JE*, 454). Pym's moral, as evidenced by the decisions of her less fortunate but more pragmatic heroines, is a tacit admonition not to care anymore. Her romantic heroines strive to renounce passion. In a less dramatic way than for Jane Eyre, they are limited in their possibilities and must cease to love their romantic heroes. Thus Deborah Wilde of *Something to Remember* chooses to be the spinster-companion with a preventive passion for her desiccated employer, a spurious attachment designed to ward off real feeling. Mildred Lathbury of *Excellent Women* embraces a marriage in which she can be useful to her husband in his anthropological research. Leonora Eyre of *The Sweet Dove Died* refuses James's overtures of peace and a reinstatement of their quasi-romantic relationship. Pym rewrites the *Jane Eyre* story in these three different variations, all directed against a reunion with a Rochester figure.

Does this caution reveal excessive pessimism about the possibility of love? As if to test this hypothesis, Pym also attempted a version of *Jane Eyre* which tentatively offers the promise of a blissful union. In *An Unsuitable Attachment* (1982), Ianthe Broome does not renounce her love for the glamorous hero but allows it to 'sweep over her like a kind of illness, "giving in" to flu' (*UA*, 147). This equation of love to sickness is a perception shared by the characters who surround the heroine and who consider her diseased in her desire for romance. Sophia, the vicar's wife who figuratively represents 'wisdom' in the novel, is even tempted to dramatically halt the marriage, in the manner of the interrupted ceremony in *Jane Eyre*. She confides to another character after the wedding that she had ' "hoped somebody might stand up at the back of the church and forbid the marriage—like in *Jane Eyre*— and expose John as an imposter. I wanted it to happen, and not only for Ianthe's *good*" ', she concludes (*UA*, 254). She dreams of a universal acknowledgement of male duplicity, in order that everyone might know what miserable creatures men are. The narrator tempers this harsh judgement against a romantic ideal: 'John was not an impostor, or no more of one than are most of the men who promise to be something they cannot possibly be' (*UA*, 254). Still, this retraction is only partial and does not cancel out Sophia's sweeping pessimism. John may not have sunk to the perfidy and deception of a Rochester, but he is none the less basically false and inferior.[7]

The marriage in *An Unsuitable Attachment* sheds a revealing light on Pym's reworking of *Jane Eyre* material. It suggests that she wanted a romantic (if unsuitable) attachment to succeed. Yet she could not fully countenance such a conclusion. Her heroines cannot give hope to plain women like Mildred Lathbury, who marry difficult men like Everard Bone, or even to plain women like Ianthe Broome who marry attractive men like John Challow. The heroines' fates are seen either as second-best or as liable to failure. Brontë's heroine renounces love only to gain it in the end, achieving a fulfilling marriage at Ferndean, however problematic this arrangement may seem. Pym's Jane Eyre heroines (except for Ianthe, herself a doubtful case) must renounce love in order not to lose what precarious peace or contentment they have.

Pym complained of not finding 'comfort' on rereading *Jane Eyre*. This quality holds a high value for her, and I think that she intended to offer it to her own readers by showing that life can be lived without the fulfilment of romantic ideals. She succeeds in this design by gently mocking her heroines' desires and by offering an acceptable alternative to dramatically conceived happy endings. She diminishes grand passions in order that the reader might receive consolation from contemplating civilized, suitable relations. Pym's novels occasionally strike a bitter, wistful note, yet at the same time they seek to offer a more realistic perspective on romance. Her fictional endings are more tenable than Brontë's because they do not dazzle the reader with as much hope for the characters' infinite bliss. Jane Eyre represents for Pym the archetypal romantic heroine, and for this reason she becomes a reference point for

Pym's characters. As if in defiance of the worst that fate can do to them, these heroines specialize in defining their own narrow lives by negation: they are 'not' like Jane Eyre. It is both comforting and infuriating.

Notes

1. A few examples of such references include the following: when Pym delivered a talk on the novelist's craft in the 1950s, she read out examples from her favourite fiction—a portion of *Jane Eyre* was among the excerpts. Pym's diaries occasionally speculate on the possibility of rewriting Brontë's novel: 'A modern version of *Jane Eyre*?' she asks, considering subjects for her next novel (*VPE*, 259). References to *Jane Eyre* appear in Pym's fiction as well. Catherine Oliphant in *Less than Angels* (1955) thinks of herself 'with a certain amount of complacency, as looking like Jane Eyre' (*LTA*, 7).
2. See Elaine Showalter, *A Literature of Their Own: British Women Novelists from Brontë to Lessing* (Princeton, NJ: Princeton University Press, 1977). Showalter also comments on the large number of Victorian imitations of *Jane Eyre* which directly followed the publication of Brontë's novel, all of which contained poor, plain, obscure governesses and dashing, cynical, Byronic heroes. She adds, 'Twentieth-century women novelists have frequently rewritten the story of Jane Eyre with endings Brontë could not have projected' (p. 123).
3. Charlotte Brontë, *Jane Eyre* (1847; rpt New York: New American Library, 1960), p. 119. Further references to *Jane Eyre* will be made in brackets within the text, preceded by *JE*.
4. See Jean Wyatt, 'A Patriarch of One's Own: *Jane Eyre* and Romantic Love', *Tulsa Studies in Women's Literature* (Dec. 1985), pp. 199–216. Wyatt argues in relation to Jane and Rochester's marriage that 'The balance of power has shifted so that their relationship no longer recapitulates, on the political surface, the asymmetries of a father–daughter relationship; yet on the personal level Rochester still embodies the patriarchal strength a girl can depend on' (p. 212). The fantasy of autonomy and adventure is carried out by the figure of St John, and thus 'The ending of *Jane Eyre* splits the human possibilities of life between the two sexes, reinstating the old gender definitions that the whole novel has demonstrated to be painfully restrictive' (p. 213).
5. Lee R. Edwards, *Psyche as Hero: Female Heroism and Fictional Form* (Middletown, Conn.: Wesleyan University Press, 1984), pp. 87, 89.
6. Sandra M. Gilbert and Susan Gubar, *The Madwoman in the Attic: The Woman Writer and the 19th Century Literary Imagination* (New Haven, Conn.: Yale University Press, 1979), p. 314.
7. Sophia's dislike of John gains further significance in light of Pym's close identification with her character. When the author's friend, Richard Roberts, wrote to her regarding an early draft of the novel, she resented

his suggestion that Sophia be scaled down in importance: 'I must have a B
Pym [sic] woman character to give my angle occasionally', she scribbled
in the margin of his letter (MS PYM 159/1, f. 20).

PART FOUR: REMINISCENCES

Though Barbara Pym remained characteristically modest about her publishing successes, her friends and acquaintances often thought of her distinctly as a novelist; they admired her because of her writing. During the many years when her work was out of favour with publishers—and her novels were out of print—she continued to have devoted fans such as Roger and Margaret Till, who eagerly searched for copies of her books. Pym's long-time friend Robert Smith wrote to her often from his various university posts in Africa to enquire after the progress of her latest novel or to exchange news of mutual friends. For some twenty-five years he and Pym met for lunches and dinners during his visits home to England. The following personal reminiscences by these people who knew her describe literary correspondences and meetings with the author. They pay tribute to her warmth, her graciousness and her wit.

Chapter 9

Remembering Barbara Pym

ROBERT SMITH

I first met Barbara Pym in 1952, soon after, I suppose, the publication of *Excellent Women*. I came to London from Cairo, where I had read and derived enormous pleasure from *Some Tame Gazelle*; this had been lent to me by her close friend from Oxford days, Robert Liddell. Accordingly I had begged him to give me an introduction to the novel's author. Barbara and I quickly discovered that we were interested in and amused by the same things. For the next six or seven years, while I was living in London, we saw a good deal of each other, meeting usually about once every week. There were many generous 'lunch hours' spent together, in relief from the tedium of our offices. Sometimes Barbara would take the Bakerloo line to meet me where I worked near Regent's Park. Then we would often eat at the Baker Street Quality Inn, famed for its imaginative descriptions of quite ordinary dishes (everything was 'topped with' this or that), and walk afterwards in that '*giardino segreto*' (for we were both Tillingites) of St John's Lodge off the Inner Circle with its statue of Hylas.[1] Other days would find us near Piccadilly Circus in the long-disappeared 'S.F.', a restaurant serving rather tiny meals, mostly things on toast, to a faithful clientele of shopping ladies and office workers. It boasted an impressive manager, who in his black coat and striped trousers looked as though he had stepped from a corridor of the Quai d'Orsay. At other times, in the evenings or at weekends, we explored the richly varied churches of London, a topic to which I return shortly.

In 1959 I left London for Nigeria, to teach at a university there, and so from then on my meetings with Barbara were confined as a rule to the university long vacations. During these years Barbara and her sister Hilary moved from Barnes to Brondesbury and ultimately to Oxfordshire. Meanwhile I was becoming something of an Africanist myself—rather to Barbara's annoyance at first, for she took a very detached view of Africa. Furthermore, now I had an official entrée to the International African Institute where she worked, and on summer afternoons I often climbed the stairs of that cobwebby building in Fetter Lane to Barbara's office in order to take her out to tea. Half seriously she would clutch a packet of cigarettes in case we met the Director, Daryll Forde, on the stairs as we returned, thus preparing an alibi ('I slipped out to buy these') which of course was never needed.

During a study leave which I spent one Michaelmas term in Oxford, we were able to meet there quite often. I recall sitting with her in the garden of Rhodes House as we wrote a joint postcard to Robert Liddell in Athens, and I described an episode which had occurred in the library that morning, which bore some resemblance to one in *Less than Angels*. Another afternoon we walked towards sunset under the blazing autumn trees of Addison's Walk. This scene, Barbara remarked, would make a splendid illustration for a card bearing the inscription 'To Wish You Well on Your Retirement'.

Meanwhile, a result of our separation for most of the year was that we exchanged letters almost every month. Barbara's letters were too good to be thrown away, so I stored them in convenient shoe boxes. But after her death they proved too poignant a possession, so now they have found a home in that great library, the Bodleian, which Barbara (and how amused she would be about this) regarded with such affectionate awe.

It could perhaps appear from Barbara's private correspondence and journals that she was a frustrated, melancholy spinster. Some reviewers of *A Very Private Eye* (1984), the recently published collection of her letters and diaries, have characterized her in this way.[2] In the years when I knew her, this was certainly untrue. She seemed to find great contentment in nearly every phase and facet of her life, especially in those 'trivial things' of which she speaks in *No Fond Return of Love* and in several of her other novels. As a writer, of course, she was indeed frustrated, yet even when disappointments over publication succeeded each other over months and years, she met the situation with her usual wry humour and irony. When, so late in the day, things changed in a dramatic way and she began to be not only published again but celebrated, she enjoyed her success to the full and without bitterness. And characteristically, at the same time she also remembered others less lucky in this way than herself.

Critical comments have been made about Barbara's attitude to religion, and since I shared so many of her churchy interests and expeditions I should like to say a little about this aspect of her life.[3] It should be remembered that these were the last years in which the Catholic religion could be *enjoyed*; before, that is, the Second Vatican Council and *aggiornamento* cast dismal shadows over not only Rome but also the Catholic movement in the Church of England. Now horror has succeeded horror: first the new literal, updated and impoverished translations of the Bible, then the etiolated liturgies and banal language of the *missa normativa* and the Alternative Service Book, and finally the endless bullying homilies from the pulpit offered on seemingly every occasion about social issues and the 'Third World'.

Before all this, religion, apart from having a greater spiritual depth, could still, *inter* a lot of *alia*, be fun. And this aspect of it we both enjoyed, while Barbara, at the same time, gladly fulfilled her obligations towards her neighbours as well as to her Church. But let me fondly recall our visits to All Saints in Notting Hill, a church famous for its carpet of flowers and herbs at Corpus Christi, for its impeccable ritual according to the precepts of Adrian Fortescue, and for the strength of its incense. In fact, the church's vicar, Father Twisaday, provided some of the quirkier aspects of the character Father Thames in *A Glass of Blessings*. In sum, let me insist that Barbara lived her life and wrote her books within a serious but never, never a solemn religious framework.

Like the senior Mrs Widmerpool from Anthony Powell's *A Dance to the Music of Time*, Barbara loved 'a chat about books', and she read—I think this is not too strong a word— voraciously. Critics have detected numerous literary 'influences' on her own writing. I am not competent to pronounce upon this topic—except to say that I have noted that Tullia Blundo in her University of Pisa thesis (1977–8) identified as influences on Barbara's writing Jane Austen (inevitably, it seems), Thackeray and Trollope, and she has also selected a passage in *Quartet in Autumn* as reminiscent of Virginia Woolf. These are rather grand names to invoke. But here I should like to mention two modern writers in whose works Barbara especially rejoiced. Studying them intently, she was prepared always to discuss them: Denton Welch and Anthony Powell. Barbara Pym and her fellow worker Hazel Holt (doubtless pausing at their desks in the Institute and seeking refreshment from arid labours over some sociological study of the pastoral Fulani, the 'law of structural drift' and other absurdities) used to set each other examinations to test their knowledge of the *Music of Time* sequence and of the Denton saga. Some of their questions came to me also in Barbara's letters.

Indeed, Barbara, rather like her character Dulcie in *No Fond Return* whom she somewhat resembled, carried out a little not too serious 'sociological research' into the life of 'darling Denton', as she referred to him. I remember too the planning of a Dentonian picnic, based on Toblerone chocolate bars and banana sandwiches. How I wish that she had lived to read the recently published unexpurgated journal and the admirable life of Denton Welch by Michael de la Noy, a work which certainly would have brought her much pleasure.

During the last months of Barbara's life I was back in London, and although she was now living in Oxfordshire I was able to see her quite often. I reproach myself that for some time I did not appreciate how ill she was and that her life was ending—yet at the same time this must have made our meetings and letters easier for us both. Almost to the last Barbara was optimistic and cheerful about her condition. In February 1979 she wrote to me that with the new drugs which were available—one, she joked, had a name like 'Tio Pepe', a favourite sherry—she hoped 'with luck' to 'have a few more years of good life'. When her health had become much worse, in October, she was similarly cheered to be told by her doctor that champagne would do more good than medication in combating her nausea.

Early in the New Year of 1980 she died. I wrote to our friend Robert Liddell after her funeral at Finstock and described the slight shock which I felt when the unexpectedly long coffin was carried into the church. 'So Barbara had the advantage of her height to the last', Robert wrote back. And for the occasion, the vicar, though by no means a High Churchman, had chosen to wear (whether by special inspiration or simply to keep out the cold of that winter day) a biretta: that splendid, Roman, angular, uncompromising, favourite headgear of the old-fashioned spikey clergyman. How Barbara would have smiled, and approved.[4]

Notes

1. Readers of E.F. Benson's *Mapp and Lucia* will recognize this phrase as referring to the 'secret garden' belonging to Miss Mapp and enjoyed by Lucia (Mrs Lucas) when she rents Mapp's house one summer in the village of Tilling. Benson's series of 'Lucia' novels were highly enjoyed by Barbara and her circle of friends, and became the source of several private jokes between us.
2. John Carey in his *Observer* review (1984) of *A Very Private Eye* makes a great point, for instance, of Barbara's penchant for graves and tombstones, and sees melancholy as typical of her character. Though she did, of course, suffer depression over various relationships and over misfortunes in publishing, her disposition seemed to me—and to all who knew her—unfailingly cheerful and courteous.
3. Victoria Glendinning's review of *A Very Private Eye* in the *New York Times Book Review* (1984) points out that Pym's journals seem to discuss religion at length but not her relationship with God. While this may be so, it certainly does not suggest the correspondingly lesser importance of religion and ritual in Barbara's life. It is possible to value something personally without writing it down.
4. These reminiscences were first given to a meeting of the PEN club in London in October 1985 and subsequently repeated to a Barbara Pym Conference at St Hilda's College, Oxford on 4–5 July 1986.

Chapter 10

Coincidence in a Bookshop

ROGER TILL

'Have you any novels by Barbara Pym?' I asked. The assistant needed further information. Giving it as best I could, I said that I was searching for novels by this writer not only for myself but for my wife. The date was 17 January 1976; the scene, a London bookshop.

Just as I had finished speaking, I heard a gentle voice behind me. Turning round, I saw two middle-aged men, one of whom smiled and said, 'I can tell you about Barbara Pym. We've just bought her old house!' He introduced himself as Luke Gertler (son of Mark Gertler, the painter). His companion was Francis Gilfoyle.

From what I had said to the bookshop assistant, Luke Gertler knew that I was eager to track down Barbara Pym's novels. Those days were difficult for her readers—before the great comeback. I had even wondered whether I should write to the author herself. This is just what I did do, when Luke Gertler had been kind enough to give me Barbara Pym's address at Finstock in Oxfordshire, where she had retired from London with her sister Hilary. In my letter I told her of the chance meeting that had enabled me to get in touch with her. I asked how many of her novels were then available and whether it was possible that others would be reprinted. I said that as a result of my searches in various parts of the country we had two of them but I had not succeeded in finding a copy of the book that my wife, Margaret, would especially like to have, *Excellent Women*.[1]

Barbara Pym replied to me in a letter dated 30 January 1976, referring to my having met the two people who had bought her London house: 'What an extraordinary thing', she wrote, adding that it seemed 'the kind of coincidence you couldn't possibly put in a novel'.

Although we made further efforts to find a copy of *Excellent Women*, these were not successful. It was a great surprise, as well as a delight, when Barbara Pym most generously sent us a spare copy that she had found. She inscribed it:

To Margaret and Roger Till
with all good wishes
from Barbara Pym
(A reward for perseverance 3.7.76)

'If you feel like making any recompense', she wrote, 'just put an extra 12s 6d (62½p?) into the church collection, or if you don't go to church, some suitable charity (cats or people)'.[2]

We continued to exchange letters with Barbara Pym during the next few years, and eventually met her on 24 August 1977. She and her sister had invited us to come and have tea with them at their cottage at Finstock on our way from Radley to Chipping Norton during a holiday. It was pouring with rain— for which reason we did not linger in the garden. Soon after we arrived, an attractive, dark-haired woman appeared, smiling broadly and saying, 'I'm Barbara Pym!' Soon afterwards we met an equally pleasant-looking and welcoming person, Barbara's sister Hilary. (We took up their suggestion that we should be on Christian name terms.) To have tea with them and to talk about books, people and places was an exhilarating experience, balanced by a repose supplied by Minerva, the cat who nestled near us.[3]

I found Barbara a less formidable person than I thought she might have been when I had spoken to her on the telephone a week or two earlier. There was considerable mobility in her facial expression and great liveliness in her talk. She often smiled. When she laughed, the laughter was sympathetic rather than satirical. Besides talking about people we had both known, we exchanged naval reminiscences. (In the Second World War Barbara had been in the Wrens, I in the Navy.) As someone who was fond of Greece, she seemed really interested to hear about the hospitality given to our son Nicholas by shepherds in their hut on Mount Ida, in Crete, and about a literary discussion they had had with him.

When our own conversation turned to literary matters, Barbara said she agreed with an elderly author of my acquaintance—the late Frank Swinnerton—when he remarked to me that a novelist, though intensely interested in the book he was writing, had little interest in it afterwards.

Looking at the books on Barbara's shelves, I saw a set of Proust's *A la Recherche du temps perdu* in C.K. Scott-Moncrieff's translation. Rachel Ferguson was one of the writers represented in a section containing some of Barbara's favourites; and I noticed Betjeman's *Ghastly Good Taste*, Angus Wilson's *Anglo-Saxon Attitudes*, a cat book, and the two volumes of the *Shorter Oxford Dictionary*. Some of the novelists who appealed to her, she said, were Virginia Woolf, L.P. Hartley and Elizabeth Taylor. When Margaret asked Barbara whether she liked Angela Thirkell, she said 'Yes'—but she thought the novels became rather snobbish later. On one of the tables there was a proof copy of one of the novels that Barbara herself had written.

When we spoke of her own work it was clear that she had no liking of the title of one of the two novels of hers which we happened to possess at that time, *No Fond Return of Love*. Telling us that that title was chosen by the publishers, she added, 'My novels are not about love—not *that* kind of love'.

When Barbara said something about 'being dishonest socially' (I think she was making no specific reference) I murmured, half-seriously, 'Yours ever'. She laughed. I wonder whether, from some dim recess in my mind, I had remembered a comment made by Mildred Lathbury, the narrator in *Excellent Women*, about a letter she was writing to Rocky Napier: 'The ending had cost me more anxious thought than was justified by the result, but I believed that "yours ever" was the correct way to finish a friendly letter to a person for whom one was supposed to have no particular feelings' (*EW*, 184).

As we were leaving the house early on that wet August evening, Barbara and Hilary came out to see us off. Their farewells were as characteristically warm as their welcome had been two hours earlier. I still have a happy memory of Barbara's firm and genial handshake.

After meeting, we continued to exchange letters. Commenting on some old literary competition entries of mine in the *New Statesman* and other papers, Barbara wrote in a letter of 26 October 1977, 'I never went in for one myself, though I did once do a parody of More's "Utopia" for the school magazine . . . I was also very interested to have some information about Allan M. Laing, who figured so much in the competitions of those days.'

In this letter, Barbara also wrote about a television programme, 'Tea with Miss Pym' (BBC 2, 21 October 1977).

> Of course they made the garden look much bigger than it really is. I liked the snap of me at a bus stop in Fleet Street—they made me go up for the day. I also liked the BM bit, illustrating an extract from *Q in A*. I'm not sure that I altogether approve of the tea drinking image; though I do like tea, I also like sherry and gin and wine but perhaps in one of my years tea is appropriate?

That gently questioning aside was reminiscent of one of her fictional characters wondering whether such and such a course of conduct would be 'suitable'. We could understand the slight misgivings Barbara had about the image presented by the title of the programme—yes, but it was Tea with Miss Pym that gave us an abiding memory of the genuine and warm-hearted person we had already sensed from her novels and letters.

Notes

1. [*Editor's note*: Margaret Till describes her first encounter with Pym's work: 'In the early 1950s when we were living in a primitive cottage in Weardale, I switched on our battery wireless set to listen to *Woman's Hour*. They were halfway through the first instalment of a serial that immediately delighted me. It was called *Excellent Women*, by Barbara Pym. I vowed not to miss any of the other instalments, and to try to get hold of the book.']
2. [*Editor's note*: Margaret Till adds, 'in the end I put the money into the box in Durham Cathedral, for which I have a special liking, and I hoped this would be all right.']
3. [*Editor's note*: Margaret Till writes, 'Barbara and her sister Hilary were younger-looking than I'd imagined. They hadn't turned into Belinda and Harriet, but had retained a more flexible view of the world and an even more refreshing sense of humour. Barbara and Roger did most of the

talking, mainly about literature. Hilary played a supporting role, though she was clearly also a person of considerable interest and ability in her own right. To Barbara, she was obviously an essential and valued companion.

I hadn't wanted to go there empty-handed, and took with me a fruit-cake, made from a very easy recipe. It's practically the only kind of cake I ever make. I sent the recipe to Barbara and Hilary afterwards, and Barbara wrote on 21 February 1978 that she had made it 'very success-fully.']

Index